How to Have a *Normal* Conversation:

20 Strategies for Productive Small Talk, Flowing Rapport, and Instant Likability

Patrick King

Social Interaction and Conversation Coach at
<u>www.PatrickKingConsulting.com</u>

Table of Contents

Introduction

Let's cut to the chase—you picked up this book because, on some level, you acknowledge that you are struggling socially, perhaps even to have just a *normal* conversation.

It may be that you're battling feelings of loneliness or disconnection, or it may be that you're confused and discouraged about how to really *talk* to people.

The good news (or is it bad news?) is that **social struggles are extremely common today.** If you find connecting to other people difficult, exhausting, or confusing sometimes—take heart, you're not abnormal!

While a little social anxiety now and then is more typical than you think, the trouble with ongoing social struggles is that they can be self-reinforcing:

- You engage socially
- You're uncomfortable
- It goes wrong
- You feel bad about it
- You decide not to engage socially anymore
- ... which means that the next time you engage socially, you feel even *more* uncomfortable

Luckily, it's possible to halt this cycle and turn things around.

In the chapters that follow I want to show you that struggling socially or finding conversations difficult does *not* mean that you're a bad person, or that people don't like you.

It also doesn't mean that you cannot change.

Instead, **social skills are just that—skills. And skills can be acquired, no matter what your capacity is today.**

A Problem-Solving Approach

When our relationships work, life works.

Connecting well to others makes us happier, healthier, and stronger.

On the other hand, feeling disconnected, awkward, unseen, unheard, lonely, detached, and unwelcome can leave us feeling awful, no matter how good the rest of our lives may be!

I'm not going to lie to you and tell you that the only reason you're having social difficulties is because of other people and what they are or are not doing. That would be an insult to your agency and free will, and it would also disempower you.

Each of us turns up to the social landscape with a different set of strengths and weaknesses. What are *you* currently working with?

- Neurodiversity
- Anxiety

- Depression
- Bad habits
- Introversion and shyness
- Social or cultural issues
- Trauma or bad experiences
- Moving, going through a breakup, or navigating a life change
- Feeling just a little socially rusty and out of practice
- Feeling like you never properly learned to socialize in the first place

Let's be pragmatic and take an honest look at exactly where we are right now—not with judgment or condemnation, but with wide open eyes and a little calm curiosity.

What follows are eight extremely common conversational mistakes that could be quietly tanking your social life.

They may seem like small things, but the small things add up.

Bad conversation habits lead to bad relationships, and bad relationships drastically reduce the quality of your life.

Almost certainly you will have observed these mistakes in other people, but my challenge to you is to **see whether you can identify them within *yourself*.**

When we face our struggles head on, with clarity and honesty (a little humor goes a long way, too), then we can begin to learn some of those skills we may be missing and gradually become the kind of socially successful people we had the potential to be all along.

As you read through these eight common social mistakes, decide for yourself how relevant the issue is for you right now.

Give yourself a rating out of ten for each one. This will help you prioritize where to place your focus, as well as help you identify potential strengths.

Mistake 1: "Boomerasking"

Reflect: Do you ever ask questions just so you can have the opportunity to answer them yourself?

Be honest!

Maybe you've framed the question so that it looks like it's about the other person, and maybe you even listen while they give their answer. But the speed with which you jump in to share your response to the questions quickly reveals your real motive.

The other person feels disregarded, understandably, and like they've been used as a prop.

So-called "boomerasking" has nothing to do with old folks—it's about asking "boomerang" questions that come right back to the asker.

> "...a sequence in which individuals first pose a question to their conversation partner ("How was your weekend?"), let their partner answer, and then answer the question themselves ("Mine was amazing!"). The boomerask starts with someone asking a question, but—like a boomerang—the question returns quickly to its source (Brooks & Yeoman, 2025, *Boomerasking: Answering Your Own Questions*)."

It's not necessarily a social faux pas to answer a question you yourself have posed; rather, people can tell when a question has been posed *solely* for that reason.

Mistake 2: Interrupting

Reflect: Do you ever cut people off before they're done talking?

Most of us don't feel like we're the interrupting type... until we're in a conversation where we have something really, really cool to share!

Interrupting isn't always a bad thing, and context matters. Different social situations tolerate varying degrees of conversational overlap, and every group has its own style.

Regardless of why we interrupt (and regardless of how amazing the thing we want to say is), interruptions usually send a simple message: "What I have to say matters more than what you have to say."

Boil it down a little more → "I matter more than you."

Understandably, people who feel de-valued this way are not in a hurry to share more of themselves—or else they may be in hurry to interrupt you back, and the conversation quickly becomes a competition.

Mistake 3: Talking about yourself too much

Reflect: Do you always make the conversation about yourself?

It's good to open up, to let other people see us, and to share our authentic selves in conversations. Truly seeing and hearing one another is the whole point of social interaction, right?

The problem is when it becomes imbalanced, and your portion of the "limelight" takes away from theirs. Do you ever talk so much about yourself that it starts to overshadow the other person or squash their contribution?

If you do this, don't worry, you're not a narcissist. In fact, it's often anxiety that makes people self-focused, and forget that the conversation is not their responsibility alone, but a shared co-creation.

Good conversations flow. It's all about the dynamic back and forth—otherwise it's more of a boring lecture than a conversation.

Mistake 4: Giving unwanted advice

Reflect: Do you love telling people what to do?

Here's some profound life advice (which you probably haven't asked for): Most people do not want you to tell them how to solve their problems. What do they want, then? That's easy. Usually, they want you to:

1. Be there
2. Listen to them while they vent a little

That's it.

Clumsy advice-giving often leaves people feeling diminished, judged, or condescended to. Yes, even if they've asked for it!

Pushing our suggestions onto people can come across as subtly trying to elevate ourselves… and it only invalidates the other person's ability to solve their own problems.

The alternative?

Listen.

Not to evaluate, identify flaws, or offer a solution, but just to hear what they have to say. Be alongside people as they unfold their own thoughts, rather than pushing yours on them. Commiserate, don't problem-solve.

Mistake 5: Asking closed questions

Reflect: Do you ask too many closed questions?

Some questions open doors.

Other questions seem to slam them shut.

- **Closed questions** - those to which a single word response will suffice, usually *yes* or *no*.
- **Open-ended questions** - the answer can be quite literally anything.

You can see which one invites the other person to open up, share, and say more... and which one shuts things down, or makes the conversation feel like a job interview or police interrogation.

Compare:

"Have you watched [popular film]?"

"What's your favorite kind of film?"

The two questions above will lead to different responses, which in turn will lead to different conversations... which over time will lead to entirely different relationships.

Think of a conversation as a joint exploration through a wide-open field—not a pre-determined path that you both have to follow.

Mistake 6: Interrogating

Reflect: Are you too forceful in conversations?

Asking too many closed questions one after the other? Yep, that can certainly make someone feel interrogated.

But interrogation is about more than just rapid-fire questions. It's about your overall demeanor and the tone you bring to social interactions. Without realizing it, some of us can approach conversation with a subtle *adversarial* or *aggressive* vibe.

Maybe we feel we need to persuade, convince, or argue a case. Maybe we feel we need to debate, explain ourselves, or prove something, when in reality, we probably just need to relax!

- Do you often talk so fast, so much, and with so much intensity that the other person feels a little bombarded or bulldozed?
- Do you often steer (even, ahem, control) the conversation to where you think it should go?
- Do you love instigating a little debate... whether the other person wants to or not?

Passion is great! High intensity people bring zest and energy to the table, and they often have plenty of value to share. The irony is that being too pushy about it can actually put people on edge and make them feel defensive. This means that they're less receptive than ever to all the amazing stuff you want to tell them.

Walls come up. Connection fizzles.

Mistake 7: Never asking follow-up questions

Reflect: Do you actually engage with and remember what people tell you?

Asking people questions is always good, but it could be argued that what matters more is *what we do with the answers we're given.*

Do you actually listen to people, and then *show them* that you've listened by asking a question that meaningfully follows from what they've told you?

Sometimes, the problem is that our questions don't go deep or far enough. We ask, wait for an answer, then ask about something unrelated. We might even keep asking the same thing repeatedly, never allowing the conversation to move beyond the shallowest level.

Conversations should deepen over time. We need to show others that we're paying attention, that we care, and that we're curious to know more.

Mistake 8: Judging, dismissing, and disrespecting

Reflect: Do you unconsciously transmit the attitude that you don't really respect the other person's point of view?

Phew. This last one can be a little hard to admit to.

We may not even realize we're doing it, but our unspoken attitudes can nevertheless leak out in our body language, posture, voice, and language.

When people feel judged, they shut down. They retreat.

If people feel that you don't take them seriously, don't value them, or don't truly respect them, a wall comes up and it may never come down again.

You might not *say* outright, "I think your perspective is inferior to mine" but sometimes thinking it is enough. Dismissive, invalidating language can be subtle… but its effects are not.

The Solution

So… how did you do?

Some of these reflection questions might have hit a little close to home… that's great! **Those are precisely the areas that hold the most potential for you and your social development.**

In the chapters that follow we'll be revisiting these eight major mistakes in more detail and exploring the deeper issues beneath them. There's *one thing* that these eight mistakes have in common.

For now, however, let's make it ultra-simple:

- **The problem?** Self-focus.
- **The solution?** Gently shifting awareness outwards again, onto other people.

No matter where you're struggling the most right now, **the way out is to reorient awareness.** When we make this all-important mindset shift, we experience:

- Less ego, more real confidence
- Less anxiety, more resilience
- Less self-absorption, more curiosity about others
- Less self-importance, more appreciation
- Less conflict, more chemistry
- Less control, more presence

Communication errors, when it really comes down to it, are nothing more than misplaced awareness, and a misunderstanding of the purpose of human interaction. If we get *this* right, then everything else will flow more easily.

Before we dive in and see exactly what this mindset shift looks like, try to answer this one question for yourself:

"What is the single most significant obstacle preventing me from enjoying a healthier social life?"

Clue: When someone offers this as a suggestion on how to improve your social life, you respond with, "Yes, but..."

Now, holding this obstacle in your mind, let's jump in and get troubleshooting.

Chapter 1: "I Just Freeze Up in Conversations."

You unexpectedly bump into someone you know out and about. You greet each other, make a comment about the weather or whatever, establish that the other one is "fine" and then… crickets.

You stand there like an idiot.

You can't think of a single thing to say. In fact, you feel like you've never had a thought in your head in your entire life. The moments creep by painfully and feel like years… you become aware of the silence and you realize you don't know where to look or what to do with your hands. If only the ground would open up and swallow you…

Sound familiar?

This excruciating social phenomenon is actually so common it has its own name: the Spotlight Effect. Because it really does feel as though you're all alone up there on a stage, the bright hot spotlights burning your eyes, and a massive crowd of people before you, all waiting for you to entertain them.

Understanding the Spotlight Effect

The truth? This phenomenon is actually a robust cognitive distortion—it's down to a **faulty misperception.**

The Spotlight Effect = overestimating how much people are judging or scrutinizing us.

The thing that may be really unexpected, however, is that this bias is not about low self-esteem. Rather, it's about what psychologists call an overarching **egocentric bias**. In other words, self-focus.

- We think that we are more visible, on display, and prominent than we are.
- We think others are more preoccupied with our flaws than they are.
- We think that others are paying more attention to us than they are.

Basically—we put ourselves at the center of our universe, and automatically assume that our perspective is the only one. We cannot imagine that people are more preoccupied with themselves and their worlds, than with noticing or judging us.

Are you someone who finds social interactions *embarrassing*? Then you'll be interested in the following research, published in the *Journal of Personality and Social Psychology:*

- Researchers asked student participants to wear Barry Manilow shirts to class, with the assumption that students would find this pretty embarrassing (for those readers younger than 60: Barry Manilow was a popular singer in the 70s).

- The researcher asked the students to estimate the percentage of people they encountered in class that noticed this embarrassing shirt. On average, they guessed that 50% of people had noticed.
- When the other students were actually interviewed, however, it was revealed that only about 25% of them had noticed the shirt (Gilovich et. al., 2000).

That's noteworthy: A self-focus can make us incorrectly guess *double* the amount of attention we receive. What's more—the 25% only "noticed" —there's nothing in the research to suggest they particularly cared.

Remember that other people have an egocentric bias, too; they're too focused on themselves to be judging and assessing you!

The big takeaway here? Often, social anxiety is about self-consciousness—which in turn is a problem of focus.

You are the one who is shining the spotlight on yourself. The scrutiny you're withering under is often your own!

The spotlight effect can interact with unhealthy social assumptions, too. For example, we may believe:

- "It's up to me to say something entertaining, impressive, funny, or charming."
- "People are actively assessing, judging, and evaluating my every move."
- "I have to work hard to win people's respect, interest, attention, or liking."
- "I am the only one responsible for the success of this conversation."

Yikes! That's enough to make anyone freeze up, right?

But these beliefs, combined with the spotlight effect, work against us. **They set us up to fail, because they make conversation a performance.**

When we are self-focused, anxious, and a little unsure of ourselves, we can put enormous pressure on ourselves to "say the right thing." We're on that stage, with bright hot stage lights shining on us.

But think about it: Isn't this quite an egocentric perspective to take?

- **Conversation is not a performance**, it's a mutual and reciprocal interaction.
- **Conversation is not about your flaws or shortcomings**, it's about your presence and willingness to connect.
- **Conversations are not tests that you have to pass to get people to like you**, they're opportunities to engage with one another.

- **Conversations are not something you give to the other person**, they're something to create and share together.

This is a humbling and stress-relieving perspective shift.

It's not all about you! What a relief.

The Solution

If you find yourself going blank in conversations, don't worry—it's normal.

Allow yourself to normalize the idea that you won't always have something witty or relevant to say on the tip of your tongue. It's not because you're boring, or you lack something, or you're doing it wrong.

Just remind yourself right there in the awkward moment: This isn't about me.

Feel uncomfortable with the spotlight on you? Well, turn the spotlight away, and onto something else.

Shift your attention outward and towards:

- The other person
- The surrounding environment
- The interaction itself

In fact, one surefire way to lower the pressure on yourself *and* make the other person feel good is to **ask questions—especially follow-up questions.**

In fact, there's very encouraging research to suggest that people are not expecting us to perform, but to engage. It's the outward shift that makes people connect to us and like us, not how well we can impress or amuse them. Karen Huang and her colleagues conclude that there is

> "...a robust and consistent relationship between question-asking and liking: people who ask more questions, particularly follow-up questions, are better liked by their conversation partners." ('It Doesn't Hurt to Ask: Question-Asking Increases Liking.' 2017, *Journal of Personality and Social Psychology*).

Ironic, isn't it? While you're stressing about what to say to get people to like you, all you really need to do is show that you like *them* enough to share a little of that spotlight.

Ask a question and a follow-up question, and you'll never run out of things to say.

Don't freeze up! You're not on stage, the clock isn't ticking, and people aren't scrutinizing you, waiting for you to mess up. Feeling this way is proof that you've slipped into that egocentric perspective and are actually less present than ever. Instead:

1. Shift focus
2. Re-engage

→ Turn the attention outward and ask a simple question to get things warm and flowing again.

Important: Huang et. al. observed that questions increased liking, despite the fact that nobody anticipated they would—indeed, people tend to underestimate the number of questions their conversation partner will tolerate.

So, ask questions—more of them than you think.

First, ask a question:

- "Man, the traffic this morning was crazy. Did you find the place OK?"
- "So, dog or cat person?"
- "Watched anything good on TV lately?"

Will these questions light anyone's world on fire? No. But what they *will* do is get that back-and-forth flowing and invite the other person to respond in a comfortable, low stakes way.

When they answer, instead of interrupting, zoning out, or jumping in to give your response to the question, ask your follow-up:

- They say, "Actually, GPS took me the strangest route—but it did get me here on time!"
  - You follow up with: "Oh really? What way did you come? You're traveling from the east, right?"
- They say, "I've got to be honest, I don't really like cats or dogs. But I do have a bird."

- o You follow up with: "A bird! I don't know why I always forget about birds. What kind of bird is it?"
- They say, "Hmm. Well, I haven't been watching TV much. Actually. at the moment I've been rewatching a bunch of old movies from my childhood..."
- o You follow up with: "Oh yeah? OK, now I'm really curious, what's your all-time favorite?"

Again, the *content* here is not what's doing the heavy lifting—it's the energy of the back-and-forth, and the quality of the attention. **You are not self-focusing, so you're alert, present, and engaged with the other person**. That means your conversation, whether shallow or deep, is going to feel good.

Follow-up question tips:

- **Keep it simple, short, and light**. Ping that tennis ball right back over the net—it keeps things lively.
- **Give the follow-up question a little "padding."** Add an expressive response ("Wow!" "Really?" "Huh.") plus a little observation or disclosure of your own ("I'm coming from that direction, too; rush hour can be pretty bad.")
- **Pay attention to what they're paying attention to.** Do they suddenly seem a tiny bit more emotionally animated? Do they

perk up at a particular question? Ask more about *that*.

Feeling a little "stage fright"? Immediately forget about yourself. Instead, think of a way to engage *externally*, connect, show interest or demonstrate that you like your conversation partner. Your anxiety will soon evaporate.

Questions and follow-up questions help, but that's not all you can do to take the pressure off:

- **Make a compliment or an observation**
  - "Nice sneakers! That's such a cool color combo."
  - "Wow, that is super neat handwriting."
  - "I really like your accent."
- **Say something about the environment**
  - "It's so busy. Is there, like, an event going on in town today?"
  - "Isn't this weather just perfect?"
  - "Looks like the 341 bus is late again!"
- **Talk about the interaction you're both having**
  - "It's so crazy bumping into you like this— what are the chances?"
  - "It's been nice chatting."
  - Even: "I'm sorry, my brain appears to be on holiday today, I think I've actually forgotten your name..."

Finally, there's one little known method of overcoming your own social awkwardness and preventing the feeling of going blank in conversations. Widen your awareness and **take notice of anyone in the social group who may be feeling like you**—a little excluded, anxious, or unsure of what to say. Then, make a warm, friendly gesture in their direction to bring them into the conversation.

This achieves two things at once. You engage and make your own contribution, take the pressure off yourself, and you also demonstrate that you are attentive, respectful, kind, and genuinely interested in others. This feels good… and it makes you *look* good!

Chapter 2: "Small Talk Feels so Shallow…"

"I'd love to meet someone special, fall in love, and maybe even get married one day… but I wish there was a way to just skip over all that boring talking and dating stuff. It's unbearable."

"I have a lifelong dream to be a really good pianist. But, ugh—piano teachers are always trying to get me to do embarrassing things like scales and fingering exercises. I keep telling them I'm not interested in that trivial stuff… I want to be a *pianist*!"

"I deserve a job role that really fulfils me, pays well, and makes use of my skills and qualifications… but engaging with potential employers is such a waste of time. Why do all this fake interview stuff when I could just be working? It's pointless. And super awkward. I'm going to skip that part."

Sounds silly, right?

Yet these are exactly the things that people say about small talk. It's:

- Boring
- Unbearable
- Embarrassing
- Trivial
- A waste of time
- Fake
- Pointless
- Awkward

- And most important of all: *optional*

We want connection, closeness, intimacy, and the joy of encountering another person—yet we want to skip over all the parts that reliably lead to that connection!

Dating doesn't get in the way of marriage; it paves the way to it.

Boring musical exercises don't detract from learning to play the piano—it's what learning to play the piano looks like.

Attending interviews isn't an unrelated, optional part of getting a job. It's *how* you get a job.

In the same way, small talk isn't some kind of inferior talk, or just an annoying part of social life that we can skip over to get to the good stuff. Small talk is *how* we get to the good stuff.

➔ That means that if we care about succeeding socially, we need to care about small talk.

Let's make some mindset adjustments so that we can approach the prospect of small talk with genuine ease, interest, and calm curiosity:

Small talk is a door.

Lightweight chit chat is an important gateway to greater intimacy, trust, and connection.

It's not important in itself, but it matters because of where it leads, and what it opens up into.

Think of it this way—there's no way to get into a room but to go through the door; likewise, there's no way to enter into a connection with someone without going through the small talk portal.

Small Talk's Magic Is Its Smallness

Do you feel like small talk is unimportant, kind of meaningless, and a little shallow?

You're right.

It's all of those things—and that's exactly what makes it so powerful!

Small talk is a first step, a tiny nudge, and **a low stakes, low-risk way to make a social gesture towards another person.** It doesn't cost anyone much, but it's a small step in the right direction.

It may feel like small talk is kind of awkward and unpleasant, but the truth is that it would be way harder—and way riskier—to launch directly into close intimacy and trust. A little like marrying any old stranger and hoping it works out!

Small talk is actually a sophisticated social technology... even if it doesn't always feel like it in the moment.

Psychologist Arthur Aron is famous for his "36 Question" study, which shows that when it comes to building new relationships, what matters is **progressive self-disclosure** (Aron et al., 1997).

There are two parts to this:

- **Self-disclosure** – Think of intimacy as a gradual increase in trust over time. And think of trust as a *reward for willfully taking on social risk.* When you self-disclose (i.e., share something personal about yourself) you risk rejection, judgment, and more. Self-disclosure costs. This means that when someone voluntarily does it, we perceive it as a sincere signal to grow closer. If that signal is seen, respected, and *reciprocated—*you're off to the races.
- **Progressive** – Intimacy is acquired by degrees, over time, step by step. There is no shortcut. There is no cheat code. It's a ladder, and you cannot climb one step without having climbed the one before it.

Aron and colleagues compiled a series of 36 questions that grow increasingly more intimate. The questions themselves are not all that important (we'll take a look at them at the end of this chapter)—**what matters is that they progress in order.**

Small talk is taking those first few steps on the ladder.

At first, you share something that's not personal at all—a remark about the weather, a comment about your weekend plans. You invite a reciprocal disclosure: "Anything nice planned for this weekend?"

But then you take the next step. You share something slightly more personal than that. Maybe you talk about a pet, a partner, or something you quite like, for example a type of food or a Netflix series. You again invite a reciprocal response by asking a question. They answer it.

Have they made a similarly sized self-disclosure? Great! Then you take the *next* step.

Slowly, step by step, you deepen intimacy by taking turns to self-disclose while also inviting self-disclosure. As you share a bit more about yourself, you simultaneously show joy and interest in them sharing a little of themselves. Done right, this process is seamless and ultra-comfortable. In other words, **people who are good at small talk actually spend the least amount of time doing it!**

Small talk opens the door. Self-disclosure is walking through it.

Important:

- **Closeness always develops in sequential stages.** Even people who turn out to be fast friends or soulmates have to start at the first step. They may move through the stages of intimacy *faster*—but nobody gets to skip a stage! Be patient.

- **Real intimacy has to be reciprocal.** You both have to climb the ladder *together*. Stay on the same step. If you self-disclose and the other person doesn't reciprocate, then don't take that next step. Otherwise, you risk overexposing yourself and regretting it later.
- **Actually take the risk.** There is no intimacy without risk, and that means being willing to be *vulnerable*. Dare to say something *slightly* contentious, unexpected, or surprising (big emphasis on *slightly*).
- **Be responsive.** Self-disclosure is important and so is acknowledging and respecting the self-disclosure of others. Pay attention to little cues that they want to take that next small step with you. Don't be judgy. Receive that disclosure with interest, respect, and warmth.
- **Have things gone south?** It's OK to fall back to the previous step sometimes. The magic of small talk is that if you do accidentally share too much or if things start to feel weird, it's not a major disaster, because you've only taken one cautious step—not a whole bunch of steps at once!
- **You don't have to climb the whole ladder.** Finally, bear in mind that relationships all differ in their degree of closeness and depth. You don't *have to* climb the whole ladder

with every person you meet. Remember that you're free *not* to reciprocate someone else's invitation to self-disclose if you're happy at the current rung of the ladder.

The Solution

Every conversation in every relationship will fall somewhere on the intimacy ladder.

As you're talking to someone, become aware of your intimacy level, and how much each of you is currently revealing about themselves.

Does the conversation feel boring, stuck, or a little too safe? It may be time to take that next step.

1. **Make a personal self-disclosure** appropriate to the level you're already at, meaning attempt to show yourself to a degree *slightly more* than has been done so far. In other words, show that you're willing to go first and take the next step.
2. **Then, invite them to do the same**. A literal question may work, or you can just make space nonverbally for them to follow suit and share a little something of themselves ("I always find the villains more interesting… how about you?")
3. **If they respond to your invitation and also self-disclose, respond with warmth.** Never make people regret opening up to you, even and especially if it's only a little thing! Show

interest, care, and respect ("OK, so you're more Disney than Marvel. I can get that!").

Pull off the above three steps and congratulations—you've taken one step on the intimacy ladder. Chill out a little before attempting the next one; better yet, wait to see if *they* initiate the next step, so things stay balanced and even.

"But I'm never going to see this person again, I don't care about *intimacy* with them."

The above steps work with *any* relationship, from a deep romance to a quick chat with someone you meet once in the waiting room at the dentist. You might only talk to someone for a few minutes, but that doesn't mean you can't take a few steps up the ladder together!

At the very least, remind yourself that using the above principles just makes social interaction more genuinely enjoyable. Are you stuck next to someone on a plane that you'd otherwise never talk to? It doesn't mean you can't make the best of the situation.

Aron's 36 Questions

Now let's take a look at Aron et. al.'s question list—notice how they gradually ratchet up in intensity, and how each question probes a little deeper the last.

- Given the choice of anyone in the world, who would you want as a dinner guest?

- Would you like to be famous? In what way?
- Before making a telephone call, do you ever rehearse what you are going to say? Why?
- What would constitute a "perfect" day for you?
- When did you last sing to yourself? To someone else?
- If you were able to live to the age of 90 and retain either the mind or body of a 30-year-old for the last 60 years of your life, which would you want?
- Do you have a secret hunch about how you will die?
- Name three things you and your partner appear to have in common.
- For what in your life do you feel most grateful?
- If you could change anything about the way you were raised, what would it be?
- Take four minutes and tell your partner your life story in as much detail as possible.
- If you could wake up tomorrow having gained any one quality or ability, what would it be?
- If a crystal ball could tell you the truth about yourself, your life, the future, or anything else, what would you want to know?
- Is there something that you've dreamed of doing for a long time? Why haven't you done it?
- What is the greatest accomplishment of your life?

- What do you value most in a friendship?
- What is your most treasured memory?
- What is your most terrible memory?
- If you knew that in one year you would die suddenly, would you change anything about the way you are now living? Why?
- What does friendship mean to you?
- What roles do love and affection play in your life?
- Alternate sharing something you consider a positive characteristic of your partner. Share a total of five items.
- How close and warm is your family? Do you feel your childhood was happier than most other people's?
- How do you feel about your relationship with your mother?
- Make three true "we" statements each. For instance, "We are both in this room feeling ..."
- Complete this sentence: "I wish I had someone with whom I could share ..."
- If you were going to become a close friend with your partner, please share what would be important for him or her to know.
- Tell your partner what you like about them; be very honest this time, saying things that you might not say to someone you've just met.
- Share with your partner an embarrassing moment in your life.

- When did you last cry in front of another person? By yourself?
- Tell your partner something that you like about them already.
- What, if anything, is too serious to be joked about?
- If you were to die this evening with no opportunity to communicate with anyone, what would you most regret not having told someone? Why haven't you told them yet?
- Your house, containing everything you own, catches fire. After saving your loved ones and pets, you have time to safely make a final dash to save any one item. What would it be? Why?
- Of all the people in your family, whose death would you find most disturbing? Why?
- Share a personal problem and ask your partner's advice on how he or she might handle it. Also, ask your partner to reflect back to you how you seem to be feeling about the problem you have chosen. *(Adapted from Audrey Monke at sunshine-parenting.com.)*

Chapter 3: "People Don't Like Me."

One major obstacle to getting people to know and like you is, ironically, the self-fulfilling prophecy of already believing that they *don't* like you.

Let's say you go out one day and hang out with a bunch of fairly new acquaintances. You chat comfortably enough, but it's a little stressful and nerve-racking. You held your own... or did you?

Later that afternoon you start replaying the meeting over and over again in your mind, and each rerun is giving you a new thing to worry about...

- Did they all secretly think that you were really weird?
- Were you actually the odd one out?
- Why did you have to say that embarrassing thing you said?!

After a good few hours of "post-event rumination" you've quietly come to the conclusion: nobody loves me, everybody hates me.

You may not even realize that you've come to this conclusion, or just how firmly you're holding onto it. In fact, you may just start rewriting history so that it fits in better with your assessment: "It was an awkward meeting, and the people there were all judging me."

Really?

This "nobody likes me" narrative can become so pervasive that it starts to shape your entire identity. You can even come to believe that there's something especially unlikeable about you in particular. You look everywhere for evidence that you are the least favorite, and you always seem to find it. You may start to point to this unlikeability as the reason why it's extra difficult for you to make friends.

The problem? *None of this narrative is remotely true.*

"Nobody likes me" may in fact be a garden-variety cognitive bias, and research by Boothby et. al. (2018) provides powerful counterevidence for the idea that people just don't like you. **Basically, the researchers found that people tend to underestimate how much others like them.**

They term this "the liking gap" and it's not unrelated to the Spotlight Effect bias: **we are overcritical of ourselves and assume that others will be, too.** In anxious self-absorption, we paint an unflattering picture of ourselves, and then assume that everyone else has painted the same picture.

➔ The remedy, as before, is to reduce self-focus.

Just like with the Spotlight Effect, we need to consciously turn our attention *outwards* and away from our own (perceived) flaws and onto the external conversation. There we may discover a host of signals we'd previously overlooked: signs that other people are genuinely enjoying our company.

Now, Boothby et. al. reliably found this bias in most people, most of the time, meaning that this bias is fairly predictable.

While it's common, the trouble with this bias is when it gets out of hand and starts to act like a self-fulfilling prophecy:

Step 1: You assume people don't like you.

Step 2: Your biased perception looks for evidence and, what do you know, finds it.

Step 3: You react by withdrawing, guarding, or even going on the offensive ("I never liked them anyway").

Step 4: You behave in ways that actually make you less likeable.

Oops. Things just got complicated.

Don't Create a Self-Fulfilling Prophecy

The above dynamic can be a hard pill to swallow, but it is sadly one of the possible consequences of unchecked social anxiety.

Thinking that we're unlikeable...

- Strangles our sense of curiosity and play
- Dulls our presence
- Encourages us to hide our light
- Pushes us to protect ourselves and assume the worst of others
- Convinces us to stay on a safe and superficial level
- Even urges us to go into passive judgment of others

Have you ever been described as "aloof"? What about "stand-offish"?

If so, this pattern may be an issue for you. You may be unwittingly feeding your own social anxiety. Even worse, you may be hiding yourself away, making it hard for others to get close. People see your wall and give you the distance you appear to be asking for... only for you to interpret that as a clear signal of their dislike.

- The bad news is that, unchallenged, this cognitive bias can have a devastating effect on your social life.
- But there is good news: **Chances are good that people actually like you a whole lot more than you think.**

And that not only means that you can stop being quite so anxious, it also means that you don't have to work so hard to win people's approval or impress them because *they probably already like you.*

The Solution

When it comes to the liking gap, it's easy: Simply commit to *not* relying on inaccurate and unhelpful assumptions about yourself.

Consciously factor in the liking gap, and tell yourself often, **"I feel like others don't like me right now, but I know that in reality, this is probably a biased interpretation."**

You're not wrong or crazy to think that people don't like you—after all, this bias is a fairly stable tendency across the population. Just acknowledge that from now on, you won't automatically act as though this thought is true, and you won't necessarily take it seriously just because you thought it.

Now, here's an important caveat:

Is it possible for some people to dislike us? Absolutely. Boothby and colleagues did not discover that everyone likes everyone. If you have ever disliked someone for no good reason, then you already know that this is always a possibility!

The research simply shows us that our own perceptions tend to contain a bias against us—and that it's worth making a gentle correction to thoughts that may come from this particular psychological blind spot.

We need to learn to take this thought "People don't like me" and moderate it slightly.

Try replacing it with:

- **"They don't know me yet."** Some people passively wait for others to show their liking and interest, *then* they make an effort to reveal themselves. This is backwards! How can people like what they don't know?
- **"I have no idea how they feel about me."** If you can't quite believe that people like you, then be content to say when you don't have enough information to call it either way. We are not mindreaders.
- **"They are not thinking of me at all."** Counter the egocentric bias and find relief in the fact that the other person may just be *neutral* about you.

Think about the people in your world that you like. Chances are, you don't make strenuous efforts to *show* them how much you like them, right? Other people are the same. They are preoccupied with their own lives. They're making assumptions, too!

How to counter the bias

- Before you head into a social situation, imagine that you know with perfect certainty that these people like and accept you. It will change your demeanor... and make you more likeable.
- Choose to consciously look for signs of interest, attention, and liking. Push the bias the other way. Can you see evidence

for the fact that people value you, even in small ways?

- Finally, recall the fundamental mindset shift that we are trying to make (that is, from **self-focus → external focus)** and encourage yourself to stop thinking about the question of likeability in the first place. Instead, be present, connect, have fun. Decide who and what *you* like. Then engage with that.

Chapter 4: "I Feel Really Anxious Around New People."

Some people can comfortably socialize for hours a day, engage happily in conversation, and even be perceived by others as thriving, confident social butterflies. There's a big caveat though: They can only do all this with *people they know*… but when it comes to strangers all their social genius flies out the window.

Being anxious around new people is not unusual and it's not really all that abnormal, either. Consider that humans evolved in social environments seldom larger than one or two hundred people (i.e., "Dunbar's number"). For most of our history here on earth, encountering strangers really *was* a rare and potentially dangerous occurrence.

This is the first thing we will bear in mind when approaching this anxiety obstacle: **It's normal to feel a little nervous when meeting strangers.**

But what if you've gone beyond "a little nervous"?

If social encounters are creating real panic for you, take heart. Just like any other conditioned fear response, social anxiety can be successfully *de*-conditioned; in fact, it may be one of the conditions most responsive to CBT (Cognitive Behavioral Therapy).

CBT gets thrown around a lot these days, but is there any evidence that it works? It turns out, quite a lot. In fact, Hofmann & Smits (2008) compiled a systematic meta-analysis of 27 different randomized placebo-controlled trials to see if CBT could really help with anxiety—social anxiety included.

Their findings? **There is very good reason to believe in the efficacy of CBT as a treatment approach for anxiety in adults.**

Anxiety experts Stefan Hofmann and Michael Otto explain,

> "Social phobia, or social anxiety disorder, is among the most common (and debilitating) of the anxiety disorders, and at any given time it effects somewhere between 3 and 5% of the US population, with similar statistics found in countries around the world. Cognitive-Behavioral Therapy (CBT) has been demonstrated to be the most effective form of treatment for social phobia..." (Hofmann & Otto, 2008. *Cognitive Behavioral Therapy for Social Anxiety Disorder: Evidence-Based and Disorder-Specific Treatment Techniques*. New York: Routledge.)

Importantly, there is a lot that falls under the CBT umbrella, but just because the overall approach has been found effective doesn't mean that it is always applied as well as it should be!

CBT is best facilitated by a trained professional. If social anxiety is *severely* impacting your wellbeing, then you may benefit most from tailored, professional support.

However, CBT principles are so simple and intuitive that there's plenty of scope for self-help—particularly if you're one of the millions of people who experience mild or moderate social anxiety.

Not everyone has access to professional therapy, and many prefer to help themselves.

If that sounds like you, let's trim away all the fluff and look at the very core idea behind evidence-based treatments for anxiety:

Avoidance reinforces anxiety. Approaching what we fear diminishes that fear.

Put another way: **Excessive, inward-turning self-focus intensifies anxiety, but externalizing your attention outward lowers its intensity** (Hofmann & Otto, 2008; Clark & Wells, 1995).

- **Fear** is not a problem, per se. Healthy fear is part of normal human physiology, and accurate fear responses help keep us safe.
- When our threat detection mechanisms *misfire*, however, and we incorrectly perceive danger where there isn't any, then we fall into the realm of **anxiety**—which

doesn't keep us safe, but limits and disempowers us.

Avoidance teaches us to escape and flee from things we perceive as dangerous but, if we do escape, and our anxiety reduces as a result, this ultimately teaches us that escape is useful and that our faulty perception was correct (even if it wasn't).

When we're socially anxious, *what are we actually afraid of?*

- People will dislike or even hate me (a bias we explored earlier).
- People will laugh at me and I'll be humiliated.
- People will ignore me and I'll feel worthless.
- People will reject me and that will hurt.
- People will judge or condemn me.
- People will see me for who I am and I'll feel exposed and vulnerable.
- People will not understand me, and I'll feel alienated and unseen.
- People will make demands of me that I can't fulfill.

If we perceive social interactions this way, then **avoid** people as a result, the temporary relief that results will teach us that all the above perceptions are actually true.

However, it is only when we resist the impulse to avoid and instead **approach** people that we can gather counterevidence that challenges and corrects the above beliefs.

You can start gathering data that teaches you a new, healthier set of beliefs: That people are not dangerous, it is safe to connect, and social situations are not automatically a threat.

Anxious around new people? Your "solution" may simply be to avoid them. You may turn down invitations, hide, withdraw, or be guarded and absent socially even though you're physically present.

- Instead, here's what will actually make you feel better: **Gradually expose yourself to your social fears, without reaching for your emotional crutches.**

In other words, we are back to our core idea. Make the perspective switch:

- **Away from yourself** (inward-turning, avoidant, defensive).
- **Towards others and the environment** (outward facing, approaching, curious, and hopeful).

Shift Your Attention

When you're socially anxious, take it as a good sign that your attention has shifted inwards, and that you are probably monitoring yourself too closely.

Awkwardness, self-consciousness, embarrassment—these are both the cause and result of self-scrutiny.

- "Am I making too much eye-contact? Am I being weird?"
- "How does my hair look? Maybe this jacket is stupid."
- "OK, quick, this is important, what am I going to say next?"
- "What's my face doing? Ugh, this is awkward."
- "I wonder how I'm coming across. Do I seem nervous?"

Remember: You feel anxious because you're hyper-self-aware... and the more anxious you are, the more there is to be hyper aware of!

Stop the spiral! Instead, shift that awareness outward and try to notice things other than yourself:

- **Notice tiny details about the people and environment around you**. Notice the texture of the other person's hat, the tiny hairs on the very edge of their left eyebrow, the exact color of the wood of the park bench you're both sitting on...
  - To take this further, see if you can anchor to the moment by identifying one sensation for each of your five senses—one thing you can see, one thing you can hear, etc.

- **Stop assessing, thinking, and preparing, and just *listen*.** Anxious self-focus preoccupies you with what you're going to say, and how you'll express yourself and appear to others. Stressful! Instead, just be there in the moment without trying to prepare for what comes next. Don't rehearse, don't prepare.
  - Actively listen to what you're told. Pay attention like you're getting tested on it afterwards—like your very life depends on catching every last word!
  - Practice paraphrasing, reflecting, and asking questions. Connect with what they're saying and set aside the need to say something interesting yourself.

The Solution

Use behavior experiments to test assumptions

Turning your attention outwards is a way to mentally approach fears rather than escape into your own mind.

But we can practice a behavioral approach, too—literally facing the things that we're afraid of, in order to challenge any inaccurate beliefs that may be limiting us.

The big idea: Deliberately engineer social situations that let you gather evidence for new beliefs. In other words, *do experiments.*

Step 1: Reflect and identify your current beliefs around social situations. One way to identify these is to notice when you're feeling panicky or like you want to escape, and then ask yourself, "What am I afraid will happen?"

- *Example: You may be afraid of meeting strangers because you worry you'll be put on the spot and be unable to say anything interesting or impressive. You may have a belief: "I have to carefully rehearse ahead of time so I have something to say, or else disaster will strike."*

Step 2: Now, let's test this belief. Is it really true that you have to rehearse and plan? Is it really true that people will see you as uninteresting and unimpressive unless you deliver a carefully prepared performance? There's only one way to find out!

- *Example: You arrange to have a few short, low stakes social encounters where you don't do anything to plan ahead, and just trust yourself to speak in the moment. This is the deliberate removal of "safety seeking behaviors" (i.e., avoidance by another name!).*

Step 3: Observe. Every time you engage in a little social experiment, you gather data. What actually happens? Does the outcome of your experiment support or undermine your core beliefs?

- *Example: You engage in very short social situations without preparing beforehand. You notice that you feel a bit awkward, but that it's nowhere near as bad as you predicted. In fact, you find yourself able to think of things to say in the moment and it doesn't end in complete disaster.*

Step 4: Keep going. Keep gathering data, keep testing your beliefs, and be willing to adjust your expectations and assumptions.

- *Example: You do four or five experiments where you observe yourself saying something completely ordinary and unimpressive—and the other person continues to respond with warmth and interest. You start to rewrite your beliefs. Maybe, after all, giving a flawless social performance isn't necessary for an interaction to unfold comfortably...*

Try "micro-exposures"

Avoidance keeps your unhealthy core beliefs intact, but behavioral experiments challenge them—and give you the opportunity to prove to yourself that you might not currently be perceiving things 100% accurately.

Another way to prove this to yourself is to engage in simple, easy, and low-stakes "micro-exposures."

Most socially anxious people hold similar core beliefs:

"I can't do it."

"Socializing is impossible."

"I don't enjoy new people."

"It's difficult to connect."

"Conversation doesn't come naturally to me."

Micro-exposures give you the chance to see that none of these things need to be true.

- **I can't do it** – In teeny, tiny ways, *do it*. Make that first move. Give yourself the goal of smiling and saying hello to three strangers when out walking. Review at the end of the day. Did things play out differently to how you predicted?
- **Socializing is impossible** – In teeny, tiny ways, go out and socialize. Be a little friendly to the barista or even ask if you can share a table with someone in a busy café. Then review. Is it really *impossible*—or is it just something you're not that comfortable with yet?
- **I don't enjoy other people** – Say yes to one teeny tiny social thing you would have avoided previously in the belief that you wouldn't enjoy it. Go out to an event, but stay just twenty minutes, or even ten. After the time passes, check in with yourself—are you really having as bad a time as you thought?
- **It's difficult to connect** – In teeny, tiny ways, reach out to people you wish you could get

closer to. Make a small self-disclosure, ask for help, or seek someone's opinion or advice. Share a trivial secret. Review what that feels like—did opening up actually damage you in any way?

- **Conversation doesn't come naturally to me** – In teeny, tiny ways, start exposing yourself to more conversations in everyday life. Challenge yourself to ask a stranger for directions or the time. Do it every day until it feels completely, utterly ordinary. Then re-appraise—is it really true that talking to people is beyond your ability?

Challenging the underlying architecture of anxiety takes time, patience, and self-compassion. Be honest with yourself and **don't lean on psychological crutches to get you through**—for example, preparing ahead of time, wearing earphones so people don't talk to you, or escaping into your smartphone whenever you feel awkward.

Teach yourself that *you can* face your social fears—and you can do it without the illusory help of a psychological safety blanket!

Chapter 5: "I Don't Want to Annoy People."

This next social obstacle is so common that most people don't even realize it's there. Our brains are apparently masters at conjuring up biases that work against us, and one repeat offender? **The persistent assumption that other people will not appreciate our social advances.**

We might think:

- People don't care about me.
- I'm on the periphery of my social group.
- Nobody messages me or reaches out.
- I never get invited out.
- I'm not on anyone's radar.
- People forget about me.

And yet, at the very same time, we talk ourselves out of checking up on others because we're worried we'll annoy them!

Silly, isn't it?

Research actually shows that people *greatly underestimate* how much others appreciate a check-in (Epley & Schroeder, 2022).

In the paper "Undersociality: Miscalibrated Social Cognition Can Inhibit Social Connection" published in the journal *Trends in Cognitive Sciences*, the authors explain:

> "Emerging research suggests that miscalibrated social cognition may create psychological barriers to connecting with

others more often. Specifically, **people may underestimate how positively others will respond to their own sociality** across a variety of social actions, including engaging in conversation, expressing appreciation, and performing acts of kindness."

There is a peculiar blind spot here. People (not just socially anxious ones!) tend to have distorted expectations around socializing. There's a weird double standard: We ourselves can feel lonely and may yearn for more social connection, yet at the same time we don't imagine that others have this yearning, too.

We imagine that we are the only ones who value sociality and struggle with it. Those other people out there? Perhaps we passively assume that they all already have the social life they want, so that any move we make towards them will be perceived as surplus, unwelcome.

So, we don't take the risk of reaching out.

We don't bother.

We hang back, say nothing.

And everyone suffers!

We create a world where everyone apparently feels lonely... but nobody feels willing to reach out. After all, while you're thinking, "Nobody ever gets in touch with me," the people around you might have decided against it because they thought you wouldn't welcome it.

Reach Out—More Than You Think You Should

The authors break this phenomenon down into three distinct parts:

- **Differential construal**
  o To construe means to *interpret*.
  o People interpret themselves and their actions through one lens, but imagine that other people are using a different lens.
  o For example, I may value warmth, humility, and kindness in friends, while simultaneously imagining that others choose friends according to their status, wealth, and appearance.
  o We imagine that other people's standards and expectations are so much more exacting and harsh than our own.
- **Uncertain responsiveness**
  o People are naturally risk averse, but we may over-estimate social risks like rejection. When we aren't sure of a person's response, most of us jump to the conclusion that it will be a bad one!
  o We imagine that people will respond to us in more negative ways than is realistic, and underestimate how much people will appreciate our social advances.
- **Asymmetric learning**
  o Because people tend to avoid social risk, they receive less feedback about positive

outcomes, reinforcing negative expectancies and making it harder to revise inaccurate beliefs.
  - Basically: If you believe people don't want to hear from you, you don't reach out. That means you never get to experience their appreciation and warmth when you do.

In short, if you've ever held back from reaching out in fear of annoying the other person—chances are your fears were unfounded.

People tend to like conversation, messages, check-ins, and spontaneous acts of kindness far more than we give them credit for. In fact, there could be people in our lives right now who desperately want to hear more from us!

Conclusion: We need to be aware of this misperception and take steps to counter it.

Feeling a little nervous about making a move towards someone socially? It may help to deliberately tell yourself: "They will probably appreciate it more than I am guessing they will."

Social media in particular can give us the impression that everyone else is living some fabulous, ultra-social life—which we would be interrupting! But remind yourself that other people can get lonely too, and that they almost always appreciate being remembered and checked on.

The Solution

- **Automate it.** Just assume that people *do* want to hear from you and create a "nudge list" with weekly/monthly reminders that tell you to periodically reach out.
  - Keep it light and low pressure. A two-sentence text or sharing a meme may be all it takes.
  - Consider the format they'd most appreciate. Your mom might like a call; your best friend may prefer a text. Whatever it is, simply make a habit of checking up on certain people following a fixed schedule.
- **Don't take it personally.** Remember that other people experience this bias, too, and cut them some slack if they're not reaching out as often as you think they should.
  - Make the first move yourself. You don't have to carry the entire relationship, but send out occasional "pings" and ask how they are.
- **Respond well when others ping you!** Bearing in mind the formidable bias against people doing so, try to appreciate it when someone takes the risk of reaching out to you.
  - Specifically say that you're pleased they reached out, even if only in a casual and low-key way. "Oh hey, what a nice surprise. It's always such a treat to hear from you."

Remember the three components the researchers uncovered and actively push against them:

- **Differential construal:** Think about how you receive and interpret people's social advances. Then imagine that it's possible that others see things through the very same lens that you do.
- **Uncertain responsiveness:** Yes, they may respond in a neutral or even negative way. But isn't it also possible that they may respond more positively than you think?
- **Asymmetric learning:** If you don't reach out to people, you can only guess how they might have responded. But if you do reach out, then you'll know for sure! Give other people the chance to prove you wrong.

Chapter 6: "I Don't Have Any Opportunities to Meet People."

Let's be frank: The modern social landscape can be pretty hazardous to navigate. Anyone who thinks that dating or meeting new friends is easy is likely talking from the privileged position of an already established network.

The truth is that the concept of "making friends" is itself quite a novel one. In the past, people didn't need to actively seek social connection the way they do now. They were simply engaged with the intact social fabric that was around them. You connected with the people in your family, the people you worked with, and the people in your general community.

As the social fabric of the modern world has changed, however, we can no longer rely on these natural social structures.

Today, people...

- Increasingly work from home, and those that work more "traditional" jobs may still stay in a job for just a few years before moving on.
- Work long hours. Wage stagnation and hustle culture leaves little time for socializing, family, or recreation.
- Emigrate and move more than ever before—often multiple times over.
- Increasingly receive their education remotely or online, rather than on campus.

- Have dating lives limited to scrolling through strangers on various paid-for apps.
- May have dozens of social media followers, yet go for days without speaking to another human in real life.
- Are increasingly likely to be estranged from their families—families which may be fractured, blended, or scattered across the globe.

Basically—**if you're finding it hard to cultivate a healthy social life,** *you're not alone, and it's not your fault.*

The bad news is that, as the natural social structures around us weaken, we need to be more deliberate in the way we create those opportunities for ourselves. We cannot passively lean on existing social structures—these may not really exist.

Let's zoom out and take an honest, practical appraisal of the situation. Rather than counting up friends and examining the state of your social network, instead get curious and ask,

"How often am I being exposed to social opportunities?"

You can be as emotionally balanced, friendly, and sociable as you like. But if you never have the chance to interact with any real-life humans? Then none of that matters.

Why You Need to "Put Yourself Out There"

Carefully consider your own daily, weekly, and monthly schedule. Look closely at how you spend every hour of every day. Quite literally—what proportion of those hours are spent in the company of other people? Think about:

- **How you work:** Is your job social or done in isolation?
- **How you relax:** Do your hobbies and interests involve other people or are they mostly done alone?
- **How you eat:** Do you share meals and mealtimes with others or is eating a solo event?
- **How you exercise:** Do you move your body in sync with other people or is health and fitness a private affair?
- **How you interact with your community:** Do you engage with real people as you move about the world, or are your interactions mostly anonymous and mediated by technology?
- **How you have fun:** Do you have opportunities to enjoy other people, or is your entertainment mostly about getting away from others?
- **How you find meaning:** Do you share beliefs, ideas, and rituals with others, or is your worldview limited to what happens privately in your own head?

- **How you solve problems:** Do you ask others for help and support, or do you deal with life's challenges more by buying things and services, or consulting the relevant system or institution?

If you feel that there aren't enough people in your world, it may not be because you lack social skills. The real underlying problem may be that there are simply not enough opportunities to meet new people—and consequently fewer chances to develop those social skills.

Isn't it strange how the world is packed with billions of people, and yet we are simultaneously experiencing a "loneliness epidemic"?

When you're struggling socially you can feel like there's nobody to talk to, and that the world is a lonely place. But there *are* people out there. Lots of them! It's just that we are all running on our own parallel tracks, right past one another, carefully avoiding crossing or overlapping.

The Solution

How do we create *more opportunities* to meet people?

Reaching out and making the effort to connect with people can be risky—not to mention time-consuming. If you're socially burnt out, it can feel easier to just throw in the towel and wait for others to come and find you.

I get it! People are flaky, everyone's busy, and it sometimes feels like you'll never find your people. If you're an introvert, neurodivergent, or socially anxious already, it can feel exhausting to keep putting yourself out there yet never feel like you're making any progress.

If you need it, here's your permission: You don't have to keep exhausting yourself this way!

Instead, **work smarter, not harder:**

- Instead of reinventing the wheel socially, so to speak, find pre-existing social groups that already have their own momentum, and join in.
- Instead of carrying the burden of continually trying to arrange new meetups and get-togethers, find groups that meet on a recurring basis.
- Instead of trying to find new friends "from scratch", find one or two—then piggyback off of *their* social network. Repeat.

Let's take a look at each idea in more detail.

Join recurrent, activity-based groups

...and attend regularly

If you rely on other people's spontaneous desire to get together, you might be waiting a long time. People are, let's be honest, kind of lazy. The best chance they have of doing anything—socializing included—is if it becomes an automatic habit.

Recurring social activities remove the strain of repeatedly trying to organize things and give you a comfortable framework. What's more, gathering around a shared activity takes the pressure off.

Friendships form with repeated exposure and familiarity. Basically, the more you see someone, the more familiar they feel. People's brains make the shortcut that familiar = friendly, and over time, friendships develop.

Pick groups, clubs, or societies that meet regularly and on a schedule. Pick those that are centered around an interest or shared activity— the more sociable the better. Consider:

- Sports or fitness groups, or things like hiking or walking groups
- Volunteer groups based around shared activities
- Choirs, bands, or dance clubs
- Book clubs, creative writing groups, chess clubs, or board game groups
- Acting clubs, debate societies, Toastmasters, stand up, slam poetry, or improv groups
- Parenting, toddler, or pet enthusiast groups
- Crafts, art, cooking, model-making, fine dining, or DIY clubs
- Even something unusual like war re-enactments, cosplay, geo-caching, wild swimming, or metal detecting groups

Things that may be enjoyable but are a little less valuable socially:

- Time limited and self-focused classes, like yoga
- Silent activities with no opportunity for discussion, such as watching movies or meditating
- Activities where you are unlikely to encounter the same people again, for example, those related to travel

Research shows that people tend to like those they see the most regularly. In other words, over time **simple familiarity leads to a feeling of comfort and friendliness** (Zajonc, 1968; Finkel et. al., 2015).

Friendships take time to develop—a lot of time. Some theorists estimate that it takes more than 200 hours of interaction to become someone's close friend (Hall, 2019).

If you try to gather these interactions from scratch each time, and orchestrate deliberate meetups for every single hour, it's going to feel forced. It's going to feel exhausting. It's going to feel like too much of a commitment.

Instead, let recurrent social activities do the heavy lifting for you. You'll rack up those precious hours, but without incurring too much social risk or exhausting yourself.

Pay attention to weak ties

Rehabilitating a broken social network (or building one that never really existed in the first place!) can feel daunting.

But it doesn't have to. **Shift your perspective and reframe your task simply as *getting your foot in the door.*** For example, if you befriend one person, you are instantly connected to their entire social network—if you play it right. Enter "weak ties."

A weak tie is a distant social connection, with which you have infrequent and more emotionally neutral interaction.

Through these weak ties we:

- Gain access to new information, ideas, and news.
- Experience other perspectives, to our benefit.
- Encounter new opportunities as they open up.
- Give us an "in" to new social circles, bubbles, and groups.

Weak ties don't just create a pathway for new professional opportunities, collaborations, or connections, they make you available to certain moments of serendipity that may have otherwise not occurred.

Sociologist Mark Granovetter, who first coined the term weak ties, explains how it's actually acquaintances and people on the periphery of your world that expose you to the greatest social prospects—it's here that your social network is growing and expanding.

That means that while it is important to make close friends, romantic partners, and deeply trusted professional connections, the health of your social life also depends on the existence of those not-so-close friends, too.

Weak ties increase the social opportunities you are exposed to—even without you knowing it. How do we increase their number?

- **Join recurring activity-based groups** and attend on a regular basis.
- **Stay open and curious**—not just about the people around you, but the people around *them*. Remember the names they mention, pay attention to the details, and politely inquire about their friends and family.
- **Offer help and support when you can.** Whether professionally or personally, make it known what value you offer in general. Are you happy to sometimes walk other people's dogs? Do you occasionally rent out a spare room? Can you act as an impromptu translator or do you have

connections in the catering industry? Make it known.

- **Gossip—properly.** Show interest in other people's lives and actively seek out new information and perspectives. This requires a good memory and genuine listening skills!
- **Share expertise and resources**. Chat to people about the work they're doing, what problems they're experiencing, and their plans for the future.
- Link people in your network to one another. **Make referrals and introductions**. This gradually builds a perception of your trustworthiness and competence.

Being aware of and making the best use of weak ties requires a certain *community mindedness.* For some of us, this comes naturally; for others, it can feel like learning a foreign language!

But be patient, be curious, and be genuinely willing to be of value to others, and in time you will create a social network that is robust and healthy. A thriving social life is like a forest ecosystem: There's a lot going on, and not everything in it is as important to you as everything else... but *everything is connected.*

Chapter 7: "I Make Friends… But They Drift Away Again."

Sure, we've all heard about the loneliness epidemic, the anxiety epidemic, and the depression epidemic.

Something that may be downstream from all of that? The *flakiness* epidemic.

Since the dramatic social fallout of the Covid lockdowns in 2020, people have been, shall we say, a lot less reliable than they used to be. Social commenters everywhere bemoan a rising trend in people bailing out of plans last minute, being noncommittal about invitations, and "ghosting". At the same time, more people than ever feel utterly burnt out, and see cancelling a social commitment as sweet, sweet relief—even an act of self-care.

And so, should you find yourself actually connecting with a new friend and getting things off the ground… you may be bitterly disappointed as you watch it all fizzle away again.

- You clearly like one another but somehow it never amounts to more.
- You both keep saying, "Let's do this again," and then never do.
- You enthusiastically tell one another how "busy" you are (really, you're not *that* busy).
- They don't take the initiative… but then again, neither do you.

A new friendship is an incredibly fragile thing. Relationships, in their own way, are like habits. Once they're firmly embedded into your everyday life, they tend to stick. But *before* they're embedded in this way? They're at risk of being sidelined or neglected.

While an established relationship can endure even very long "dry spells", a new one cannot. Without enough initial care, attention, and momentum, new connections will shrivel. For example:

1. You meet a friend of a friend, hit it off, and hang out a few times. It's great!
2. You invite them to hang out again one day. They call it off at the last minute.
3. A week or two (or three) goes by, and they invite you out. This time *you* flake.
4. At this point, things are starting to feel like a chore. Life is busy. You both push it to the back of your minds. A few more weeks go by.
5. Now it's feeling *really awkward*. You both keep meaning to "catch up."
6. You don't.
7. A few more weeks go by...

What's really happening here? You're both mutually ghosting one another, and before long, the whole thing dies a quiet, but certain death.

It might not look like it, but the story above is a bona fide *tragedy*.

Promising new connections fail not because the people involved are mean, or because they don't sincerely like one another, or because nobody wants it to happen. This budding friendship dies like a tender seedling that just never got the chance to set down proper roots.

It dies because of a lack of consistent, mutual initiative.

Your Flakiness Survival Protocol

Navigating an increasingly complex and fractured social landscape takes self-awareness, strategy, and a lot of courage!

Thriving socially in a world that sometimes makes connection difficult takes energy and conscious effort—but it can be done. The first step? **Be realistic about obstacles and challenges, and commit to doing your best anyway.**

We can break it down rather simply:

1. Don't flake
2. Don't be bothered by others who flake

Let's consider the easy one first: **Don't let other people's unreliability get you down**—what's more, don't allow *their* lack of commitment and sociability to set *your* standard for the same.

- **Try not to get discouraged.** The world can be an exhausting place, and many people may simply not have the capacity to be as present socially as you'd like. Don't take it personally. Don't let it dishearten you. It's simply not in your control.

- o What *is* in your control? Your own behavior. More on that in the next section.

- **Be patient and accommodating... to a point.** People are only human. That means that they will require a degree of understanding, forgiveness, grace, and kindness. However, it's important not to be overly obliging to people who *consistently* disrespect your time, those who are *consistently* unreceptive to your advances, and those who *consistently* demonstrate an unwillingness to make time for you.

- o We all need to draw a line in the sand. Where? That's up to you.

- o Example: You may set up a "three strikes" rule where you overlook cancelled plans or declined invitations three consecutive times... but then you pull back and wait for them to reciprocate.

- **Know when to move on.** It can be exhausting (and hard on your self-esteem!) to chase people who are willfully withdrawing or excluding themselves. People may be struggling emotionally, burnt out, overcommitted, or just in a life stage where socializing is not a priority. Figure out what *your* hard limits are. Then be ready to move on.

- **Refocus.** Notice the people who *are* making an effort—and lean into those relationships. Is somebody continually inviting you out, messaging you, or trying to include you? Prioritize them.

Well, so much for dealing with other people's lack of social enthusiasm. Let's turn our attention to something a little trickier, but far more in our control: our own flakiness.

The Solution

The mindset shift here is a subtle but super important one.

We need to gently challenge the assumption that socializing should always feel easy, low-, or no-effort, instantly rewarding, and convenient.

Deciding to cancel plans or even failing to make plans in the first place is a *choice*—and it's one you make after weighing up the social costs and benefits. You may tally up the costs of getting ready, leaving the house, arranging transport, spending money, and navigating a potentially stressful social situation... and ultimately decide that it's "not worth it."

Hey, it may not be.

BUT, if you value connection to other human beings and yearn for deep, healthy bonds with them, then know, realistically, *that it doesn't happen on its own*. It takes active effort and conscious investment on your part.

Like anything else in life, **being out of practice makes it so much harder to start back up again.** The more you withdraw, the harder it is to re-engage again. This is why it's so, so important to gently push yourself to get out there and make the effort, *even though* at first it may not feel easy, or effortless, or instantly rewarding, or convenient.

Be honest with yourself. Many people claim they hate being lonely and want friends… but refuse to take a single positive action in that direction, choosing instead to stay at home in sweatpants.

Are you guilty of being a flake?

Have you noticed a pattern where your promising new friendships fizzle and fade?

Then consciously choose to make a new commitment to yourself: That you will **make the effort.** Promise not to get too comfortable in your excuses, and don't let bowing out socially become a habit.

Today, certain social media trends have almost elevated introversion to the status of a morally superior lifestyle choice. Endless introspection is in; social consideration and cooperation is out. But you can buck the trend! You can choose not to valorize being a social slob.

- **Don't flake.** It's normal to sometimes not feel up to a social commitment. Expect it. Go anyway. Keep your word. Hold yourself to a higher standard. In a world where inconsideration is the norm, stand out as a person who makes the effort.
  - You may be tempted to tell yourself that you won't be missed anyway, and that it's not really important that you go. But remember Epley & Schroeder? People underestimate how much their sociality means to others. Consider others and don't let them down.
- **Be real.** Again, it's *normal* to feel a little nervous, apprehensive, or unmotivated before a social event. But if you're consistently dreading *every* interaction, ask why.
  - Are you imposing certain social commitments on yourself just because you feel you should? Out of habit, guilt, or obligation?
  - Are you forcing yourself to perform socially? Consider—what do you actually want to do? Be honest about who you want to spend time with, how often, and in what scenarios.
- **Cancel gracefully.** Sometimes you have to drop out. If so, take responsibility for immediately re-scheduling. As far as possible, find a way to keep the continuity going. If you can't make the party, can you just come for half an hour? If you can't make

Tuesday, can you make Monday? Demonstrate willingness.

- o Relationships are built on trust, familiarity, and continuity. Remember that every time you stand people up or cancel last minute, you're communicating that you will accept this behavior from them. This creates an atmosphere where nobody feels like they owe anyone anything... with predictable results.
- o Be honest (but kind) when you're just not feeling up to something, rather than making excuses. Respect it when others tell you the same. It's OK to sit one out sometimes. Just be honest and take clear steps to demonstrate that you still value that connection. "I'm a little burnt out after this week at work, can we give this evening a skip? I love our hang outs though and still want to meet up... will you be around tomorrow?"
- **Be intentional**. Don't leave it up to chance and whim to reach out to others—connection is unlikely to happen by accident! Instead, use *implementation intentions* to make your social gestures habitual and even automatic. For example:
- o "If it's Sunday morning, I'll send a message to the three friends I haven't heard from the longest."

- o "If I'm in a coffee shop alone, instead of scrolling on my phone, I'll work on an email for my long-distance friend."
- o "If it's lunch time, I'll go into the break room and see if anyone wants to chat."
- o Meta-analyses show these "if-then" plans significantly increase follow-through (Gollwitzer & Sheeran, 2006).
- o You can also automate reaching out with habit stacking by attaching your social gestures to habits you already do. For example, every day when you walk home from work, you give a friend a call—cycling through your social group one friend at a time.

- **Be mindful about your communication style.** Sometimes, new friends drift simply because they haven't found a comfortable way to connect. Maybe you're a daily text kind of person and they prefer longer, more infrequent voice calls. Maybe you like a firm schedule but they're more spontaneous. Maybe you always reach out in the morning when they're most emotionally available in the evenings. You get the idea.
  - o Be considerate of how people prefer to communicate, and how often. Don't make any assumptions—ask!
  - o Pay attention if someone seems interested but is slow to respond to texts or messages—they may just be digitally overwhelmed. It may make more sense to

arrange routine in-person meetups that
don't require any additional mental strain to
plan.

Chapter 8: "Conversations Always Feel One-Sided."

Conversation is flow.

It's dynamic back-and-forth.

A conversation is a living, breathing thing—and like anything that breathes, it's about the interplay between the inhale *and* the exhale!

Many of us face a surprisingly difficult obstacle when it comes to conversation. We either:

1. dominate and talk too much (and feel bad about it afterwards), or
2. we barely contribute at all (and feel bad about it afterwards)

Knowing that conversations should be give-and-take in theory doesn't necessarily make it easy in practice.

What gives?

Scratch the surface of any one-sided conversation and you may find deeper imbalances—not just in each person's speaking time, but in their respective

- Expectations
- Style and tone
- Value contribution
- Overall energy exchange

In other words, one-sided conversations are about misalignment—and that

misalignment concerns much more than just words!

Much "post-event rumination" centers around regrets over how much you think you spoke— either too much or too little. The key word here, though, is "think".

Our *perceptions* of how much space and time we're taking up in any interaction may not always be accurate. What's more, time spent speaking is not in itself always a perfect indicator of the balance and reciprocity of a conversation.

Exhibit A: Consider how some people may not contribute much verbally, but their presence alone brings an enormous emotional and energetic contribution to the interaction.

- Think about a cute baby or a celebrity sitting at the next table in the coffee shop. They don't have to speak much or even be involved in a conversation to heavily influence it!

Exhibit B: Consider also how a person may be perceived as contributing greatly to a conversation if they're bringing something of enormous value.

- Someone offering just the right answer or solution, much-needed advice, or help may use very few words yet nevertheless "carry" more than their fair share of the conversation.

Exhibit C: Consider that someone may be completely dominating a conversation—speaking as much as 95% of the time. But in certain contexts, it just works. If the other person is supplying plenty of encouragement, appreciation, and even goading, then the conversation will not *feel* like a selfish performance, but rather a fun and enjoyable co-creation.

In short, conversations can feel lopsided for many reasons—and talking too much or too little is just one of them.

A few questions to ask yourself:

- What were my expectations of the conversation? Are those expectations reasonable? Might they be different from the expectations of the other people involved?
- What is my conversational style like when I'm happy, relaxed, and comfortable? Am I naturally talkative? Or do I prefer to contribute in other ways? Am I expressing myself well according to my natural preferences and strengths?
- Being honest, am I contributing too little to the conversation? Too much? (Note—this is not just *verbal* contribution, but overall value; consider the energy, attention,

presence, and emotional atmosphere you bring to the exchange).

- Am I expecting too much of myself? Or too much of others? Am I carrying too much responsibility or expecting others to carry more than their fair share?

The Solution

Taking things even further, we need to understand that our intuitions about how much we *should* be speaking are also not necessarily true.

Low self-esteem, anxiety, shyness, or plain old social conditioning can convince us that people will like us more if we talk less. Some people—women in particular—may be socially conditioned to be quiet and attentive, listening more than they speak.

Without even realizing it, we may reflexively put ourselves in the position of the supportive, value-neutral listener. People who listen and cede the conversational floor, we may assume, are more likeable.

But is that really true?

Research psychologists have asked this very question, and the answer they found is pretty surprising.

Hirschi and colleagues (2022) found that **most people estimate that they should speak a little less than half the time in a conversation**

(around 45%) if they want to be perceived as likeable. They call this guess the *reticence bias.*

So far so good.

But the researchers actually put this prediction to the test, and discovered that, contrary to expectations, **the more people spoke, the more their conversation partners tended to like them** ("Speak Up! Mistaken Beliefs About How Much to Talk in Conversations." *Personality and Social Psychology Bulletin*).

The conclusion the authors came to? Speak up!

If you want to make a good impression with someone new, and to come across as likeable as possible, then your best strategy is to talk—more than you might assume. The researchers' various studies found that **people were perceived as likeable even when they spoke up to 70% of the time.** That's a lot of leeway!

Playing it safe and not speaking up might actually backfire in unexpected ways. People may indeed feel that you're being polite and they may enjoy getting to speak more than you... but that doesn't necessarily translate to them *liking you.*

OK, let's pull all these ideas together.

- Good conversations are always *balanced, dynamic, and flowing.*

- Good conversations are about *equal contribution*—but there are plenty of ways to contribute besides verbally.
- When it comes to verbal contribution, choose to deliberately counteract the reticence bias, and *speak more than you think you should.*

And now, a big caveat. What about all those people who feel embarrassed because they spoke too much in a conversation? Well, **it's possible to speak too much—while contributing too little.**

Let me explain.

"Speaking up" does *not* mean:

- dominating,
- interrupting,
- anxiously performing,
- hogging attention,
- desperately trying to impress or entertain, or
- lecturing and speechifying—

these things are actually not contributions at all. They're drains and demands on other people's patience and goodwill. By speaking too much in this way, we actually contribute too little.

Instead, "speaking up" is about making that balanced, dynamic, and flowing **contribution**:

- You inject energy and liveliness into the conversation.
- You demonstrate that you're engaged, responsive, and deriving enjoyment from the conversation and the other person's contribution.
- You show that you're paying attention and are receptive to what you're hearing.
- You show yourself to be a present and alert conversation partner—one who is actively responding to what they hear.
- You convey a sense of confidence and ease in yourself.

The cure for talking too much and talking too little is the same: contribute more.

Share a little of yourself. Offer your opinions and perspectives and let people know in small ways, who you are. Ask questions and listen carefully to the answers. React to the conversation. Be fully present. Show up. Allow yourself to become animated or engaged. Make space for that reciprocal contribution to unfold.

In other words, don't tell yourself that you need to be a safer, quieter, more restrained version of yourself in order to be liked—the opposite is true!

Remember: **It's not about how much you *talk*, it's about how much you *contribute* (but you should probably talk more anyway!).**

Chapter 9: "I'm Bad at Reading Social Cues."

Do you ever feel like you...

- Misinterpret people's body language
- Misunderstand tone and implied meaning
- Fail to catch jokes or hints
- Misjudge how people are actually feeling
- Make mistakes with timing or offer suggestions that accidentally offend or confuse people?

You may be right to home in on these difficulties as a serious obstacle to good social rapport. However, if you're already recognizing these patterns? Then that's a good thing—because it means that you're probably more socially aware than you know.

First things first: It's possible to have weak or poorly developed skills around reading social cues *without* something like neurodiversity coming into play. So, if this is an area of concern for you, don't worry—there's no reason to conclude that something's going wrong.

Secondly: Learning to better read such cues is not unlike learning to read anything else—it first requires a basic social literacy, and then consistent practice as you take those skills out into the natural social landscape.

The most important thing, however, is adopting a growth mindset. In other words, wherever your current skill level, believe that you *can* learn to do more.

This is not just optimism, but an evidence-based position: Controlled clinical studies have shown that *structured practice* in reading emotions (for example, recognizing micro-expressions) can measurably improve a person's ability to read social cues… which in turn improves relationships (Schlegel et al., 2017).

Schlegel and colleagues were interested in the effectiveness of a "short computer-based training for 14 different emotions using audiovisual clips of emotional expressions." Their results?

→ On average, the 532 participants measured showed significantly improved facial, vocal, and audiovisual emotion recognition compared to control groups who did not work through the training program.

Interestingly, the researchers noted an exception—adults above the age of 59 years did not show any benefit, possibly because they required a longer or more interactive training program than their younger counterparts.

But Wait… What IS a Social Cue?

It may be more accurate to ask, what *isn't*?

Social cues are anything that a person might use to convey meaning, either:

- Verbally or nonverbally
- Consciously or unconsciously
- In a universal or culture-specific way

For now, let's focus on nonverbal communication, since this is where meaning might be conveyed in subtle or ambiguous ways. It's not possible to provide a comprehensive list of every tiny thing that counts as a nonverbal social cue, but it may be helpful to start paying attention to *where* these cues might normally come from.

Meaning might be conveyed in:

- Facial expressions
- Body language
- Eye contact
- Vocal quality
- Proximity
- Physical touch
- Physical appearance
- Gestures and movements

Learning to become "socially literate" and reading the meaning that people embed in their nonverbal communication takes practice and awareness.

Step 1: Turn your attention outward.

Step 2: Carefully notice the way people use their faces, voices, and bodies. Think in very basic terms:

- **Open vs. closed**
- **Constricted vs. relaxed**
- **Heavy vs. light**
- **Advancing vs. retreating**
- **Movement vs. stillness**

Step 3: Consider your observations in the situational context and make a guess about what you're reading in this specific situation.

Step 4 (optional): You can gently test your hypothesis by asking questions or making comments and observing the reaction.

Here's an example of how that might look. Let's say you're at a casual get together and have started chatting to a guy you've never met before. Despite feeling a little anxious, you gently remind yourself to turn your awareness outwards and start to notice what you can.

You ask him a pretty standard question about the work he does. This is the verbal message he sends you:

"Works OK, it's great. Actually, I'm between jobs right now. You know what it's like. I'm weighing up a few options. It's great though. Exciting times."

But what about the nonverbal message? You notice:

- **Facial expression** – His mouth and jaw seem pulled tight, and his eyes are giving an impression of heaviness.
- **Body language** – His arms are held across his body; his fists are kind of clenched.
- **Eye contact** – He's looking away and to the floor. You try to make eye contact but it's like he's not wanting it.
- **Vocal quality** – Hard to say. You notice that he keeps saying "it's great," but the voice doesn't seem to match somehow.
- **Proximity** – Normal.
- **Physical touch** – None.
- **Physical appearance** – A quick scan and you see that he's possibly in his late 30s, a little overweight, and dressed more formally than anyone else at the get-together.
- **Gesture and movement** – Very little. He gives the impression of stiffness, even rigidity.

Now, all of the above observations can be made in a matter of a few seconds, if that. But when you pay attention to them in this way, a picture starts to form. You asked him about his job, and his nonverbal response was one of slight tightness, guardedness, stiffness, and avoidance. You also notice, with interest, that this nonverbal message doesn't quite align with the verbal message. For whatever reason, this guy is not saying exactly what he feels.

As he talks, you wonder: Might this guy be feeling uncomfortable talking about work? Might there be some stress around unemployment? And what's with the suit and tie—is he still working? Job hunting? Maybe he's *not* doing any of these things, and that's precisely why it's so important to him to keep wearing that suit and tie anyway...

So, what do you do with all this data? You choose *not* to ask a question about his work.

Instead, you change the topic entirely and start talking about something completely un-stressful: pets. Instantly, you notice that his body language, facial expression, and gestures relax and open up.. So, you ask him more follow-up questions on the pet topic—does he have any pets?

Now the conversation is flowing in a completely different direction!

Congratulations! You have just *read the social situation correctly* and navigated the conversation with ease and grace. You had a hypothesis, tested it, and used the result to fine tune your approach. And you can keep doing this all through the rest of the conversation. It's a tiny thing, but it will earn you some major trust and likeability points!

Had you failed to turn attention outwards, and ignored all those little social cues, you might have trapped yourself in a long, awkward conversation about job hunting—one that might have left you feeling confused, annoyed, or exhausted. Instead, you paid attention to the deeper meaning the guy was expressing—the meaning that went beyond his words.

In this way, one social cue at a time, you learn to become more socially perceptive, more present, and more conversationally intelligent (and as a happy side effect, you'll probably have a lot more fun, too!).

The Solution

The most important thing to recognize is that no matter how bad you feel you currently are with reading social cues, improvement *is* possible.

Let's start with an important perspective switch:

- Stop saying things like, "I'm bad at reading social cues."
- Start saying things like, "I'm still learning. With practice I'm getting better."

Unfortunately, we don't have access to a structured training program. Fortunately, we have access to the best laboratory in which to learn naturally: real life.

Once you remove the barrier of your own self-limiting beliefs ("I can't read people, it's just not who I am.") you can get to work learning how to better navigate your social landscape.

It will take time and consistent effort, yes. But it is a problem that can be solved.

- **Flex your powers of observation.** Are you bad at reading social cues or are you just not paying attention to them? We've already seen the power of turning attention *outwards*. Practice noticing more.
  - Look (unobtrusively) at people's faces— especially the eyes and mouth. Are they lifted or lowered? Expansive or contracting?
  - Look (unobtrusively) at their bodies. Notice broadly if their posture is open or closed. Dynamic or still.
  - While watching TV shows or movies, pause occasionally and challenge yourself to notice what people are doing with their faces and bodies. What are their voices like? You might like to take a moment to literally mimic them, then guess how they might be feeling based on how you feel when doing the same.
  - Practice in the mirror. Sometimes, we can forget that *our* faces are sending a message, too. Experiment with deliberate expressions—you may need to train yourself to convey the message you want.
- **Piggyback on other more socially aware people.** You can go a long way to reading a

social situation by simply noticing how *others* are reading it.

- o If someone is telling a story or anecdote, quickly glance around to see how others are responding, then subtly adopt their facial expression or gestures.
- o Look for patterns. Can you see consistent links between certain words, facial expressions, emotions, behaviors, and verbal cues? Pay attention to how people routinely respond, for example, to the sharing of good news. Higher pitched voices? Raised eyebrows? Gather this data like a scientist. The next time someone shares good news, try this response and see what happens.
- **Seek out trustworthy feedback.** There can be a lot of weird and uncomfortable feelings around admitting that you have trouble with social cues. Nobody likes to feel left out. The truth is, however, that people love to be helpful and supportive in this area, and will almost always respond graciously when asked for help, feedback, and guidance.
- o Ask a close friend to provide some kind but constructive feedback on subtle social behaviors you might introduce—and where there's room for improvement.
- o Seek professional help. A properly trained therapist can walk you through certain social skills step by step, in a safe and predictable environment.

- **Take it step by step.** When you learned to read, you started with the alphabet, then read simple words, then sentences, then worked your way up to full books. It's the same with social skills.
  - Start small, and practice one skill at a time to prevent overwhelm. Be patient with yourself.
  - When you feel like you've made progress, pause to celebrate and reflect on what worked and why.
- **Don't be afraid to ask!** If you're finding yourself fumbling in a social interaction, and you're not sure how someone feels or what meaning they're communicating—just ask. There is no rule to say that you have to guess all the time!
  - Ask a follow-up question, cautiously paraphrase or check, "Do I understand you?" or "Did I get that right?" You can also simply echo the emotion words they're already telling you. When you reflect, you give the other person an opportunity to correct you.
  - While you're still practicing, don't be afraid to lean more on verbal communication while you improve your interpretation of the nonverbal. You might like to get yourself an "emotion wheel" or a comprehensive list of feeling words. Get familiar with it. Practice labeling emotions when you detect them in yourself or others, for example, "Do

you think you're feeling *disappointed*?" You'll be showing empathy but also strengthening your emotional literacy.

What if you're not feeling ready to experiment in everyday life? Well, luckily there are plenty of online resources available to help improve emotion recognition.

Chapter 10: "People Think I'm Being Rude… but I'm Not!"

In this section we'll be discussing what may be the saddest and most ironic consequence of social anxiety and poor people skills. Read the following story and see if you can relate:

> *You are in a strange, new social situation, and nerves are running high. You feel pretty awkward, but you're doing your best not to show it. You smile, you chat, and you're polite. Internally, though, you're screaming, "This is a complete disaster! Get me out of here!"*

> *You leave that social situation feeling like a soldier who's survived a war. You're tired, feeling bad about the whole thing, and starting to worry. Did everyone secretly hate you? You start ruminating and looking for evidence that you were the odd one out, and everyone could tell. You really resent how badly your shyness is impacting your life…*

> *It comes as a HUGE surprise, then, when you later accidentally overhear someone discussing their first impressions of you. "She was a little rude" they say. "I don't know why she's so cold with people. Like she thinks she's better than us."*

That people have read your *shyness* as *rudeness* has got to be one of the most painful social realizations. But it's one that's worth addressing, because the fallout can be severe.

While you are feeling:

- Anxious
- Vulnerable
- Threatened
- Unwelcome
- Awkward

You may be sending strong (if unintentional) signals to others that you are:

- Unimpressed
- Aloof or detached
- Irritated or annoyed
- Stand-offish
- Judgmental

This is a real shame, but it's also not that surprising. Let's look back at our story. Remember the part where you're screaming internally, "Get me out of here!"? That's a pretty powerful vibe to be carrying in any social situation!

Even if we feel like we're being polite, friendly, and sociable, the truth is that our true feelings always leak out one way or another. **People may rightly observe that you're uncomfortable, but they don't know why.** All they see is a person who has detached and seems not to be enjoying the social environment... i.e., *them*.

Hard not to take that personally, right?

A vicious cycle emerges.

- You feel awkward and anxious.
- You turn inward, become guarded, and give the impression of not wanting to be there.
- People notice this and misread it.
- They respond to what they think is you being rude, aloof, or superior.
- You notice their reaction and, big surprise, it makes you feel even more awkward and anxious!

The end result of such a dynamic can be almost comical. One person bemoans the fact that "Nobody in the group likes me!" while the group is bewildered: "But you clearly don't even want to be part of the group!"

It's difficult, but if we're socially anxious and struggling with shyness, we need to **be aware of this phenomenon and take steps to prevent it.** It's tempting to try and hide social anxiety, be polite, and put on a mask, but this strategy can backfire when people misread it all as coldness and disinterest.

What's the way out?

The Solution

We need to actively signal warmth, interest, and liking—even when we're feeling anxious and awkward.

If you're feeling vulnerable, you may put up energetic and nonverbal shields to protect yourself. The trouble is, this can make you hard to read or even convey an attitude of judgment and dislike that isn't really there.

If you're feeling unwelcome, awkward, and even mildly threatened, your entire aura takes on a feeling of discomfort, which can easily be misconstrued as a lack of interest, dismissiveness, or haughtiness.

In other words, you may pull back out of fear, but to those who don't know what's going on in your head, *all they see is the pulling back*. They see you disengage, stand back, and shut down.

To counterbalance this, we need to be explicit and direct:

- **Express your happiness and gratitude to be there. Literally!** Remember that every human being yearns for acknowledgment, validation, and appreciation. In our anxiety we can forget that other people also crave positive feedback from us.
  - **Don't expect people to read your mind.** Don't assume they already know what you feel. Say out loud that you appreciate the invitation, that you're glad to be meeting up, that you're happy to see them, that you value your conversations, etc. Cheesy? Kind of. But it's a little vulnerability that will spare you a lot of misunderstanding later.
  - **Give compliments.** Notice where people have made an effort and praise the effort.

- o **Say thank you and mean it.** Show genuine appreciation and gratitude when people are kind or simply thank them for making the effort to arrange a social event. Research shows expressions of gratitude strengthen relationships significantly (Algoe, 2012).
- o **Remember and use people's names.** Follow up on the things they tell you and show an interest in what they're saying. Pay attention. People might not register that you're anxious... all they can see is that you're distracted and not really listening to them.
- **Be considerate.** There's no nice way to say it, but sometimes anxiety and social ineptitude can make us a little... selfish.
- o **Remember to reciprocate.** Socializing is difficult for everyone sometimes, even those who appear to be social butterflies. If you're anxious, you might miss the fact that it's your turn to host or make the next move.
- o **Shift out of self-consciousness.** Anxiety asks, "How am I coming across? What will others think? Do they like me?" Instead ask, "How are they feeling right now? What do they need? How might they be interpreting my behavior, from their perspective?" It may seem fine to arrive late to a group event... until you consider how it might make others feel.
- **Be honest.** If you are anxious but desperately trying to hide it, people may not

register the smile on your face, but the desperation behind it. They will sense that you are not really present and not being fully real. They will feel that something is being hidden—because it is!

- o **Acknowledge anxiety, don't ignore it.** It's OK to say, "I'm a bit nervous today" or "I sometimes find it hard to chat to new people." Others will now have a more accurate frame through which to interpret your behavior—you're not being a jerk, you're just feeling a little uncomfortable! People tend to trust honest vulnerability far more than fake strength.
- o **Correct yourself.** Have you just put your foot in it? Said something awkward or potentially offensive? Immediately acknowledge and apologize. Being able to laugh at yourself shows confidence and resilience. "Sorry, that was a dumb thing to say, wasn't it? I think my brain gets hijacked sometimes!" Then move swiftly on.

It's OK to be socially anxious. It's OK to feel awkward sometimes. But it's also a necessary skill to clearly signal that to others, and to **convey a friendly intention, even if we are feeling a little uncomfortable.**

We reassure others in this way not just to make them feel better (although that's a big part of it) but to stop the vicious cycle and to make our own lives easier. Make the effort to signal warmth, even if it feels a little too obvious at first. This softens awkward moments and allows others to read you correctly—as someone who wants to be there.

"I Just Tell it Like it Is"

- "Their wedding was really trashy. What? I'm just saying what everyone else is thinking."
- "God, old folks are boring. Just being honest."
- "I think I'm probably out of your league. Sorry, just telling it like it is."

Before we conclude this section, it's worth considering the "I call a spade a spade" phenomenon.

As we've seen, shyness and social awkwardness is often misconstrued as bad manners.

But what about when it really *is* just bad manners?

Enter the person who loudly claims that they're just "calling it as I see it."

This is the communication style that masquerades as brave and honest, but is often just thinly veiled stubbornness, a lack of empathy, and a refusal to observe ordinary rules of social etiquette.

If you're constantly defending yourself with the above phrase, it may be time for some

honest self-reflection. Insecurity, poor social skills, and black-and-white thinking can mean it's easier just to say what we like and conclude that if others don't like it, it's their problem.

But it isn't. It's very much our problem.

Some people genuinely struggle with reading social cues, navigating conversations, and understanding others' emotions. Other people *can* do all these things—but choose not to. This attitude can stem from complex and deep-seated beliefs about social dominance and control, self-expression, and empathy.

If this sounds like it may be an issue for you, ask yourself a few questions:

- **Do you have issues with impulsiveness in general?** Have you struggled with anger? If so, you might need to work on self-regulation, delayed gratification, and learning to be more deliberate and strategic in what you say.
- **Do you feel inadequate?** Sometimes, it can feel like we need to show up in social situations as knowledgeable, competent, and 100% sure of ourselves. This may even manifest as needing to control what others think. Consider where you might have learned this belief, and if it's still serving you.
- **Are you really the only one with access to "how it is"?** If we express personal opinions, interpretations, and preferences as absolute

truth, we risk coming across as ignorant—not to mention we may miss opportunities to learn better.

- **Are you deliberately hurting others?** It's convenient to hide behind the idea that what hurts is *the truth*, not our telling it. But is that always the case? It takes enormous courage and maturity to admit when we're voluntarily choosing to be unkind, cruel, harsh, or disrespectful.
- **Are you offering a way to make anything better?** If you're not providing any solutions or help, then "telling it like it is" is little more than an exercise in passive complaining, criticism, and negativity.

Ultimately, these are hard questions, and only you can answer them for yourself.

Truth matters and always will.

But the *way* we tell the truth matters, too, especially if we value harmony, empathy, community, and understanding.

If you've earned yourself a reputation for being a bit blunt, you might like to adopt a new habit. Before you say something, ask yourself:

1. Is it actually true?
2. Is it useful or helpful?
3. Is it kind?
4. Does it need to be said?
5. Does it need to be said by me?

6. Does it need to be said right now?

If you can honestly answer yes to all six of those questions, then by all means, tell it like it is. If not, it may be that holding your tongue is the better social move. Being authentic and expressing yourself honestly is a wonderful thing. But our feelings are not all that matter, and "telling" is not the only action we can perform in a social situation.

Forcefully sharing our opinions with others won't do a thing to change *their* opinions, and lecturing people is never an effective way to get closer to them. Pausing, reflecting, and responding with mature compassion doesn't cost anything nor does it diminish anyone—in fact, it's the single most effective way to get people to actually listen to you!

Chapter 11: "I'm Always Forgetting Names and Details."

A: "Hey, how is your wife doing? When's the due date again?"

B: "Oh, uh, she's had the baby already. Two months ago…"

A: "Shoot! That's right, I remember."

B: "Yeah. I told you all about the christening we were planning…?"

A: "(gulp) Yes, yes of course! How's little Theodore? Is he sleeping well?"

B: "It's, uh, Theodora. She's great."

A: "…"

Hear that? That's the sound of a perfectly ordinary conversation catching fire, crashing to the ground, and exploding into a million burning pieces.

Some of us really do have poor memories and forget important details—but it's not because we don't care. Nevertheless, **forgetting the things people tell us can seriously erode feelings of trust and connection.**

It takes a little effort, but there are plenty of effective ways to make sure that we're not just paying attention to what people share with us, but actively demonstrating that we've heard, and that we care about what we've heard.

There is nothing little about remembering "little" details.

To understand just how important they really are, turn the tables and recall how it felt the last time someone spelt your name wrong, forgot a central detail about your life, or evidently wasn't listening when you told them something important.

How did you feel?

Unimportant.

When someone feels that the details of their lives are irrelevant, insignificant, and not worth bothering with, then it's only a small jump for them to feel that *they* aren't seen as important, either. Even though it might not be 100% fair or accurate, people do make a reasonable assumption: *If something matters, people will remember it.*

The Solution

Realistically, there are a few reasons you might routinely fail to remember important information. Let's consider the first one:

- You genuinely don't care.

Frankly, the world is a noisy place, and we may simply not have the mental bandwidth to hang onto every tiny detail. However, you probably *do* think it's important to avoid awkward conversations, and prevent people thinking you're a jerk. In that case, **learning to better recall small details is simply something you do to make your own life easier**, and to navigate conversations that might otherwise stall.

Another reason?

- You really *do* care, but somehow all that information just goes into your head and flies right out again.

Memory is not some passive, inbuilt capacity—it's also the *deliberate choices* we make and the habits we engage in to help ourselves hold onto important information.

Consider: One person remembers their friend's birthday, and the other doesn't. These two people don't have different memory capacities, though—one just chose to set a reminder on their calendar, and the other didn't.

A final reason is especially important:

- Because you were anxious when someone first shared the information with you, you didn't properly attend to it and never formed that memory in the first place.

To encode a new memory, you need to consciously attend to that incoming stimulus. **If you're preoccupied internally with your own anxious experience, you might completely miss that information**. This phenomenon is technically not a question of poor memory, but of poor attention—you don't remember what happened because, in a way, *you weren't there when it happened.*

If your memory falls into this latter category, then you may find that when you…

- Increase mindfulness
- Reduce stress levels
- Improve presence
- Turn attention outwards

…then your memory for small details magically improves as well.

There are countless proven memory strategies out there, and every single one of them can be applied to the social landscape.

The right memory tool can help you remember people's names, how to spell and pronounce those names, important dates like birthdays and anniversaries, relevant facts like the work they do, where they're from, or where they live, little details like quirks and preferences, the stories they've told you, and their upcoming plans.

That said, a memory tool can only do all this if you actually use it!

Encoding strategies that work

To improve your memory for social details, **focus on the encoding—not the retrieval.** In other words, pay attention to what you do when you first encounter a new bit of information. That's because by the time you're asking yourself to recall it, the memorization process is already complete, and it's too late!

Here are some ideas, with everyday examples.

- **Say it out loud.** When someone shares something new with you, literally repeat it out loud (don't be too obvious about it, though— even quiet whispering can help). You're more likely to remember things that you speak out loud. It's the "production effect"—the memory you actively *create* will be more distinctive and multisensory, making it easier to put into long term memory storage.
  - Example: When you hear someone's name, echo it: "Alex! That's such a cool name, I've always liked it."
  - Tip: If you forget someone's name mid-conversation, you can sometimes get away with asking them to repeat it because you want to confirm the pronunciation (obviously, this won't work for Lee, Bob, and Sue!)
- **Practice active recall.** It can sometimes help to make yourself remember a detail as soon as possible after you learn it—in the very same conversation, if you can.
  - Example: You get home from a social event and quickly drill through the names and key details of the people you've just met, exactly as you would after an important lecture. "OK, so Bob works in insurance and his wife is from

New Zealand, Lee is in his third year at med school, and Sue has just had gallbladder surgery."

- **Use follow-up questions to engage.** It's always easier to remember stories and strings of connected ideas, than it is to remember raw data. When people share things with you, ask a follow-up question that drills down into a particular detail. Focus on the emotion of what's shared, the narrative, and the *why* of the story.
  - Example: Sue is telling you about her surgery, and you ask follow-up questions—when, where, how, and why. In the process, you not only learn additional useful information (she works as a nurse and had the op at her own hospital), but you'll flesh out these facts with richer, contextual detail that makes it easier to remember.
- **Mnemonic devices.** Good wait staff everywhere know that the key to remembering people's orders is to use memory devices called mnemonics, for example "The girl with the pink scarf gets the strawberry milkshake." Use rhymes, acronyms, imagery, or funny associations to remember key details. The funnier, more absurd, or striking these are, the better!
  - Example: You notice that Bob in insurance is kind of *old* and think it's funny that his wife is from *New* Zealand. You might visualize Lee as "Doctor Lee" in your head and imagine that he

has a little radio on his shoulder to help you remember his field—radiology.

- **Elaboration and self-referencing.** The egocentric bias does have some benefits: It's easier to remember things if we can relate them back to ourselves! Try to connect new information to yourself somehow and even elaborate on that information to make it more personally meaningful and relevant.
  - **Example:** To help you remember a friend's birthday, you could compare their birthday (October 22nd) to yours (August 20th). That's two days and two months more than you—since you will always remember your own birthday, now you'll always remember theirs. You can also remember an important year by connecting it to an event you're not likely to forget: "She was pregnant at my wedding, so that means her child must now be..."
- **Write things out**. It may seem extreme, but if your memory really is a sieve, then there's no shame in compiling careful written notes to help you keep track. Those in highly social professions know that they won't cope without a little "cheat sheet" of everyone they know. You could compile a brief profile of everyone you meet, including name, where you met them, what's going on in their lives, and what you last spoke about—even their pictures, if you're bad at putting names to faces.

- Before you go to a meeting or social event, quickly go through these details to prompt your memory. This will also give you something to talk about and let people know that you care and are paying attention. "Hey Sue! How are you recovering from your surgery? I hear it can take a while."
- **Use habit-based planning.** Using "if-then" intentions can help you cement new habits with more consistency (Gollwitzer & Sheeran, 2006).
  - Example: "Every time I'm done with a social interaction, I go home and make a note of some things I can ask about the next time I see that person. Every time I plan for a social interaction, I check my notes to prepare one or two comments or questions."

Thes tips and tricks may seem quite labor-intensive and even artificial, but their results can be impressive.

Have you ever been chatting to someone when they randomly mentioned something you told them weeks ago? Perhaps they recalled some small detail you thought nobody cared about, or asked you a thoughtful follow-up question about something that nobody else has bothered to show an interest in.

Chances are you felt quite... special.

Not only were they obviously paying attention the first time round, but they cared enough to follow through and demonstrated clear interest by returning to this point. This kind of care and attention simply cannot be faked, and when done right, it makes the recipient feel like a million dollars.

One final tip: People may throw dozens of facts and details your way, but don't worry—you don't have to remember everything. What *should* you remember? Pay close attention—not to what seems important to you, but what seems important to them.

- Do they suddenly seem a little more animated?
- Do you notice a sudden increase in their energy or emotion?
- Are they using verbal cues to tell you that a certain detail is significant?

That's your cue. Listen closely and people will shine a spotlight on the things that *they* value most, and which they want you to pay attention to.

Chapter 12: "I Struggle in Group Conversations."

"I just prefer talking one-on-one..."

I get it. Group conversations can completely confuse and discourage people.

Maybe you wait patiently while others talk, but when it's your turn, someone else jumps in and talks over you.

You hate interrupting, but feel like *you* keep getting interrupted, and the by the time you get a chance to speak, the topic has moved on, or else people are not really paying attention anymore.

Annoying.

For introverts, quiet folk, and people who aren't "loud", this can feel unfair and frustrating—as though conversations are some kind of violent contact sport, or that the only way to be heard is to be a clown.

Maybe you do speak up and say something, but people literally don't hear you, or you find your question, joke, or comment dying an embarrassing death as it appears that nobody is responding to it. Have you ever made a funny quip, only to have the person next to you repeat it... and only *then* everyone laughs?

It sucks.

Eventually, you feel so disheartened that you just zone out and let it all wash over you. You're invisible but not willing to fight to be seen.

Sound familiar?

You're not alone!

Group conversations require a different set of skills than one-on-one conversations— often, skills that seem at odds with one another!

If you feel like group chats move too fast and too boisterously for you to find a way in, relax. You don't have to radically change your personality or become a domineering loudmouth to make it work. But you *do* have to change your approach a little.

The Solution

Though it feels hopeless in the moment, there's actually a lot you can do to combat this annoying social dynamic. Let's consider each potential solution in turn.

Solution 1: Join activity-first groups

Some group discussions are lively (read: chaotic) but pay attention and you'll see that chaos is largely verbal. Instead, **try to join conversations that are anchored in activity.**

When you're sharing a group rhythm, jumping in to talk can feel a lot more natural. Importantly, these groups should be focused on activity-first—that means that the activity takes precedence, and communication emerges around it. For example:

- Any team sport
- Intensive gaming, puzzling, and problem solving
- Dancing, mountaineering, horse-riding
- Collaborative work like acting, crafting, cooking, or building

Behavioral synchrony (e.g., moving, singing, or exercising together) increases bonding and cooperation (Wiltermuth & Heath, 2009). That means you can interact socially and feel included and connected without the constant verbal sparring and jostling.

Solution 2: Adjust your expectations

When someone cuts you off or nobody notices your joke, it's hard not to take it personally. But if you can pay close attention to everything else that's happening in the group, you'll often see that you're actually not the only one to be cut off! In group situations, interruptions are often not intended nor perceived as rudely as in one-on-one situations.

Group chats will almost never be deep, calm, and balanced.

They jump from topic to topic, they're volatile, and they're often lopsided. But we only stress ourselves out expecting them to be what they can't be. Instead, embrace the excitable and, yes, shallow energy that group dynamics can bring, and don't be too ready to assume that it's because you're boring, unlikeable, or unimportant.

This leads us to the next solution...

Solution 3: Buck up!

We might be overlooked more than others because, paradoxically, we're carrying ourselves in a way that makes us easy to overlook!

- We speak too quietly
- We are too reluctant and timid
- We passively wait for permission or an invitation to share
- The unconscious message we communicate is: "I'm sorry! I know I shouldn't be talking so please forgive me!"

Once we let go of the expectation that groups are going to patiently take turns so that everyone gets a chance, then it can feel easier to be slightly more robust and demanding ourselves.

Keep reminding yourself that **conversational rules for groups are different than for one-on-one.**

Group conversation skills are a little like stage makeup: In normal light, it seems garish and over the top; however, on stage *it needs to be that obvious* in order to be properly seen.

It's the same thing with your communication style—you're not changing who you are, you're just making things a lot more obvious so you can be fully and clearly seen as the person you are.

- Turn up the volume a little.
- Sit tall, breathe, and open your diaphragm. Lift your chin. Project yourself.
- Be a bit pushier than you think you need to be.
- Make your body language, articulation, and facial expression just a little more exaggerated than you normally would.

It may feel awkward at first, but truthfully, this slight amplification is just right. Don't think, "Why should I have to force myself to be heard?" Just think of yourself as needing to don a little stage makeup. "I'm making all this a little louder and clearer so the people at the back can hear me!"

Solution 3: Find groups with better communication cultures

People talking over one another, shouting, interrupting, chaos... some groups are just like that.

Whether it's down to culture, age, gender, or simply the way a family conducts themselves, you may never gel with a particular social group. Sometimes, people are dismissive of those they genuinely believe to be lower status—and sadly there's little you can do about that.

Being old in a younger group?

Female in an all-boys' club?

A foreigner who doesn't catch all the cultural references?

It can be hard.

But you have permission to forego those groups and find your own tribe instead! Don't stress yourself out trying to fit in with what genuinely seems to you like self-absorption, rudeness, or rotten communication skills. Instead, invest your energy in finding your own people (more on that later).

Solution 4: Keep alert

You might not like it, but it's often better to think of group conversations as a children's party game instead of a civilized, carefully choreographed debate.

- **Stay engaged** and give the impression of listening attentively as others speak. Lean in. React to what you're hearing. Match the overall energy and mood of the group.
- **Pay close attention to the right place to jump in**. This is an instinct to develop over time, but pay attention to the overall flow and rhythm, and introduce your contribution at a natural break. Use body language and gestures to signal, "Ooh, I have

something to say!" to give people a chance to make an opening for you.

- **When you speak, be loud enough to hear.** If people don't hear, don't get flustered and sulk; just repeat yourself.
- **Actually sit *with* the group**, preferably somewhere central, and don't hide off to the side or behind a potted plant.
- **When you do get a chance to speak, be bold and *take* it.** Hold the floor. Don't drone on or be overly hesitant, and be more concise than you would in a one-on-one conversation. Make it very clear what your central point is, and when you've finished. Then hand the conversation over.

Solution 5: Be graceful about it

Getting talked over happens to everyone from time to time. What should you do if someone is domineering or rudely interrupting?

- **Raise your voice** (important: That doesn't mean *get angry*, it just means *increase your volume)* and continue talking. Avoiding eye contact with the interrupter can sometimes help, too.
- Say something like,
  o "Oh, I was still talking, just a second," or
  o "Whoa, can I finish?"
  → This is delivered in a neutral, good-natured way; the tone you'd use to politely tell a cashier that they'd given you the wrong change.

- **Use body language or facial expressions to assert yourself.** Raise a hand or a finger, or else give them *that look.*
- Still being talked over? It can happen, no matter how well you play it. **Whatever you do, don't sulk, withdraw, or get nasty.** Stay in the conversation. Group chats are dynamic things—the energy will eventually shift again, and you can try to catch the next wave.

Solution 6: Use groups as a springboard

Don't really enjoy the group vibe?

There's no law that says you have to!

However, knowing that group situations are excellent opportunities to encounter lots of new people socially, it may be worth putting up with the group dynamic now and then, so you can meet people to hang out with later, one-on-one.

The thing is, all the qualities that make group conversations difficult, like…

- The chaos
- The shallowness
- The jostling for attention
- The speed at which they move
- The disjointedness

… are precisely the qualities that make them ideal for engaging with new people in a light, low stakes way.

Use social groups as a springboard. Identify people you like, then engage with them a little in the group context to gauge their interest. Depending on their response, you can then invite them to do something outside of the group.

It doesn't take off? That's OK. You can fall back to interacting with them in the group context again—which will mercifully be shallow and fast moving enough for it not to matter!

Chapter 13: "Networking Feels Fake to Me."

- Do you cringe at the prospect of delivering your so-called "elevator speech" to random people you've just met?
- Does the idea of self-promotion leave you cold?
- Is your social world filled with people who have no idea what you do for a living, what projects you're working on, or what your talents and skills are?

For many, the entire concept of networking is alien and super uncomfortable. As a result, they avoid it entirely, choosing to fly under the radar rather than risk the awkwardness.

At the root of this discomfort lies a perspective that might not be entirely accurate: **the tendency to view networking as transactional**.

And transactional = bad, right?

It's as though we imagine that good relationships are those that are natural, spontaneous, and purely for their own sake... but bad relationships are those in which people are deliberately trying to *get something* out of one another. And that's kind of... gross.

Socially adept people can sometimes stumble with professional networking because they feel weird navigating situations that feel exchange-based, conditional, and goal-oriented.

"Professional" socializing can almost seem like a contradiction in terms. It feels embarrassing to engage with people when you suspect they may be quietly keeping score in the background. It can feel even more awkward to have to *be* that person!

If this kind of thing rings a bell for you, then don't worry. Many people find professional networking even more loathsome than small talk—and that's saying something!

However, a slight mindset shift may shed some interesting light on this entire phenomenon. **It makes sense to be skeptical of networking when you mentally frame it as *transactional*.** But what happens when you frame it differently—what happens when you put *gratitude* at the center?

The Find, Remind, and Bind Theory

Sarah Algoe (2012) was the first to put forward the Find, Remind, and Bind framework. In her paper published in the journal *Social and Personality Psychology Compass*, Algoe explains that **gratitude has a profound function in building and maintaining social relationships—professional ones included.**

The role of gratitude is threefold:

- It helps us **find** potential partners, friends, and allies.

- It helps **remind** us of the existence of current relationships and their value.
- It helps **bind** us more strongly to those existing relationships, deepening, and securing them over time.

Thinking in terms of gratitude can help counter the limiting view of networking as transactional. According to Algoe, gratitude towards someone who helps you is actually the fuel that fires more beneficial encounters, eventually setting off a cycle of mutual responsiveness.

Networking, then, is just the first step—the first input of the gratitude fuel to get the cycle going.

How does all this theory apply to professional networking in particular?

Find. Gratitude helps you identify people who are already being generous with their time and insights. Gratitude becomes like a kind of filter or flashlight that lets you locate potential in your social environment.

- Instead of: "What's in it for me?"
- Think: "How can I be more attuned to the potentially altruistic acts and supportive behaviors already available from others?"

Remind. Gratitude helps you appreciate the relationships you currently have, and all the ways they are supporting, nurturing, and benefitting you. Gratitude becomes like a helpful reality check. It recalibrates you so that you don't take certain things for granted.

- Instead of: "What can I get out of people?"
- Think: "What am I already getting?"

There's another aspect to "remind"—*we can remind others of our existence and our value.*

- Instead of: "How am I going to sell myself to this person?"
- Think: "How can I remind them of the value I already bring?"

Bind. Expressing gratitude helps tie people together. A favor is received and appreciated, the giver feels good, and the receiver is momentarily more attentive to the relationship, now more willing to reciprocate.

When people who give are thanked and appreciated, they feel understood, valued, cared for, and important. Not only does this rewarding feeling compel them to do more for others, but it also primes them to receive reciprocal gestures with gratitude themselves. Plenty of warm fuzzies result!

- Instead of: "They only scratch my back because I scratch theirs."
- Think: "Collaboration is enjoyable."

Networking is not about transactions, but about establishing as many satisfying, mutually beneficial connections as possible. **Being**

guided by gratitude is a way to be authentic AND strategic.

Gratitude helps you spot opportunities in your environment.

Gratitude helps you maintain and cultivate value in your social network.

Gratitude sets up reinforcing loops of collaboration.

The Solution

While those who hate networking would rather die than make cheesy pitches to strangers, there's one thing that's far easier: *thanking people.*

Showing appreciation.

Asking for advice.

Praising a job well done.

These things don't feel like your stereotypical networking moves, but that's exactly what they are: prosocial gestures that will strengthen rapport, trust, and liking.

True networking is relational, not transactional.

Here's how to do it:

- **Be genuinely thankful and appreciative.** Trying to get something from someone you barely know and who doesn't owe you anything can feel awkward and embarrassing. Instead, think of any relationship—personal or professional—as something that necessarily grows over time. Start by making a few small goodwill deposits:

- o Thank people for their time and effort, even if it's only for tiny things. Demonstrate that you value their contribution. For example, approach a lecturer or speaker but don't ask for anything or go into promotion-mode—just introduce yourself and express thanks for their insight.
- o Of course, be sincere! Careless flattery is a waste of your time and theirs.
- **Give praise—but be specific.** A genuine compliment is an excellent and totally natural way to begin a one-on-one conversation. To really get an "in", though, make a comment that is thoughtful, unique, and likely to be well-received by that person in particular.
- o You might follow up with a thoughtful question. "That is such an interesting perspective, I've never thought of it that way before. Mind if I ask what inspired you to take that approach?"
- o Asking for a favor can feel rude, and asking for help can feel embarrassing. But asking for *advice* is a different game entirely. One of the best ways to ask for a job, for funding, for support, etc. is to ask for someone's

advice on how to get it. They'll be more willing to engage.

- **Be generous and be helpful**. The power of the *small* helpful gesture is that you can make it without coming across as manipulative or calculating. Be generous and freely offer people a little resource or tip that will have them unconsciously taking you out of the "neutral" category and placing you in the "positive" category.
- Introduce people in your network, give someone a great review or referral, or share a useful bit of information or news with them, without expecting anything in return. You never know what the outcome will be, or the form it may take.

If the idea of networking makes your blood run cold, consciously reframe it as the **skillful use of gratitude to establish, grow, and maintain a healthy social network.** Much less intimidating, right?

Don't know enough people? Use gratitude to **find** them. Look around at people who are already offering their time, giving their expertise, or hosting relevant events. Cast your net far and wide, be curious and ask about those weak ties in your existing network that you may need to connect with. Be grateful for them—and express that gratitude.

Made a few new promising connections but don't know what to do next? **Remind** yourself to cultivate that relationship and continuously express gratitude. Give a compliment, praise something specific, ask for advice or feedback, or just pose a sincere question (one of the most flattering things you can do for people is to show real interest in and respect for their expertise).

On the other hand, don't be afraid to bring yourself to people's attention, and remind them that you're there. Reach out and share something useful. You're not asking them for anything—you're *giving*.

Has someone done you a favor, helped you out, or shown an interest? Lock in those gains and **bind** that growing connection with gratitude. Offer sincere thanks and gratitude and find a meaningful way to reciprocate. Keep those connections alive.

Networking is about gradually building rapport and trust. Like any relationship, it takes time, so be patient and be willing to let it go when something just isn't lining up.

Be friendly, warm, and lead with curiosity and generosity. Don't force anything. Celebrate when you've made a new link! Hold onto that person. Then be curious about who else in *their* network you can get acquainted with...

Chapter 14: "I Get Stuck at Acquaintance Level."

For some of us, *making* friends is the easy part—the hard part is *keeping* them.

If you've been struggling socially and working hard to learn how to reach out, connect, and launch new friendships, it can be a little bewildering to realize that hitting it off with someone is just the *first step*. What then?!

See if you can relate to any of the following:

- You easily make new contacts, but none of them really progress into something more.
- You have loads of acquaintances and casual friends, but nobody you'd feel comfortable asking for help in an emergency.
- You've got an impressive friend *group*, but nobody you feel able to hang out with one-on-one.
- You know how to get people to like you, but you wonder if they'd still like you if they knew you any better...

People who are socially anxious can often get hung up on the very early stages of relationship formation—because that's where they tend have the most trouble! They scarcely think about what happens *after* they break the ice and make that coveted connection, and that means they're often unprepared and unpracticed in the work of **cultivating** those relationships.

If this sounds like you, then your challenge is to **make the switch from connecting to progressing**.

The seed is planted.

Now it's time to get on with the work of watering that seedling, nurturing it, and giving it the space, time, and care it needs to grow and thrive.

Think Cooking, Not Chemistry

When you add potassium to water, it explodes, hisses, and shoots along the water's surface like a tiny car burning with a purple flame. This is chemistry: Two things come together, and a reaction occurs, all by itself.

Interpersonal chemistry happens, too. Who knows why, but occasionally we are blessed to meet people and experience an instant spark with them, a zing, a "click" of recognition... perhaps even an explosion of purple flame.

It's effortless, and it's exciting. You understand one another. You get on like potassium and water.

However, chemistry (at least the interpersonal kind) is *just a first step*.

Natural compatibility is wonderful, but we need a little something extra. After all, nothing at all will happen between potassium and water if they never make the time to be in the same place as one another, right?

Instead, **think of relationships as cooking, not chemistry.**

Coconut and lime were made for one another, apple and cinnamon are a match made in heaven, and there is a special and ancient alchemy between garlic and ginger. However, all these things need to be *carefully and consciously brought together* for the magic to happen.

Cooking, not chemistry.

Good relationships may *start* with chemistry, but without **conscious and progressive effort**, they'll quickly end. They can fizzle out or get stuck forever at acquaintance level.

Cooking is a deeper, slower, and more deliberate form of chemistry. It's the process whereby we build rapport, trust, and liking over time.

The ingredients:

- Repeated positive interactions.
- Mutual responsiveness.
- Reciprocated trust/disclosure cycles.

Mix all these together and let them marinade and stew over *time*—because time is the final secret ingredient.

Many of us fail to progress our friendships because we fail to recognize the deliberate steps we need to take to move it from one stage, to the next, to the next. Just as a meal doesn't spontaneously assemble itself by magic, neither does a good friendship develop with zero intentional effort to *make* it develop.

The Solution

You need to **escalate**.

While most people don't mind if professional relationships plateau at a particular level, personal relationships should ideally always be growing and evolving, even if only in tiny ways.

However, here's the mindset shift: You cannot rely on shared interests, good intentions, or even high natural compatibility to carry a new relationship.

What does deepen a connection? Self-disclosure.

In other words, we need to take the risk of showing a little more of ourselves to someone.

Let's look at what the research says.

Cho & Toma published a fascinating 2022 paper titled, "An Experiment on the Effects of Self-disclosure on Perceived Partner Responsiveness and Intimacy in Zero-Acquaintance Relationships."

They paired up sets of complete strangers, then varied how much each participant self-disclosed (either with high or low intensity). Next, they asked participants to rate how responsive they felt their conversation partner to be, and the degree of intimacy they experienced.

The results? High intensity self-disclosure led to higher perceived partner responsiveness, which in turn increased feelings of intimacy.

It turns out that self-disclosure leads to feelings of closeness but *mediated through* **perceived responsiveness**. In other words, self-disclosure acts as a bridge. It allows people to feel understood, cared for, heard, and trusted. It allows them to feel that others are *responding* to them. It's this that leads to feelings of intimacy.

Another study (McCarthy et. al., 2017) suggests that people that measure high in self-esteem and agreeableness tend to engage more in emotional self-disclosure. For these people, **trust** is the bridge that leads to more intimacy.

In short, high self-esteem + agreeableness → greater trust → more vulnerable disclosure → increased intimacy.

On the other hand, Sparrevohn and Rapee (2009) found that those with higher social anxiety disclosed less, expressed fewer emotions, and consequently reported lower intimacy.

So, social anxiety → lower trust → less vulnerable disclosure → reduced intimacy.

Where does self-disclosure fit?

- People who disclose more are liked and trusted more
- People disclose more to those they like and trust

Self-disclosure doesn't just express intimacy; it creates it. The more you share with someone, the more you like one another, and the more you like one another, the more you share. The entire process is mediated by mutual responsiveness and reciprocal trust.

Step 1: Initial self-disclosure. You open up a little and reveal something personal about yourself. This is a slight risk you take, which automatically demonstrates goodwill and a degree of preliminary trust in the other person.

Step 2: Perceived responsiveness and trust. If your disclosure is met with understanding, respect, empathy, and acceptance, then trust deepens a little.

Step 3: Reciprocity. A kind acknowledgement of the emotional risk incurred in your self-disclosure may prompt them to make a disclosure of their own. The risk is balanced, and the gesture recognized.

Step 5: Further disclosure. Over time, repeated cycles of disclosure and trust invite further, deeper disclosures on both sides. Intimacy is the fruit of trust—it's the depth of enjoyment that becomes possible when you're with someone you know you can trust.

Step 6: Feedback loop and ever-increasing intimacy. As you take turns disclosing and respecting one another's self-disclosures, you are demonstrating responsiveness and building trust. This creates a feedback loop that naturally progresses and helps develop relationships.

From the above it should be clear: if a connection feels like it's stalling or fizzling out, what may be missing is that first crucial step – someone needs to take the risk of an initial self-disclosure. Why shouldn't that someone be you?

There are plenty of reasons we may be unconsciously holding back and limiting our own social success:

- **We're afraid** of actually being *seen* as the people we are—we're afraid of being vulnerable and authentic.
- **We're people-pleasers** and have conditioned ourselves to center the other person—while inadvertently removing ourselves from the equation.
- **We've been hurt or disappointed before** and are unwilling to take the risk again— even if it's small. Rejection is painful, and some of us have sadly had negative responses to disclosure in the past (we'll explore this more later).

- **We have low self-esteem** and deep down just don't think that people are all that interested in us—especially the ugly parts!

Unfortunately, hanging back in this way means that we keep people at arm's length. We may genuinely want more intimacy, but at the same time we place artificial limits on how close we are willing to let people get, and how much we are willing to let them know.

Luckily, the "risk" involved is in reality very, very small. That's the beauty of taking your time—if you self-disclose gently and gradually, you're never really in any emotional danger. **Rather, you are extending a good-natured invitation to someone, an invitation to take one small step forward together**—and hoping they respond positively.

Self-disclosure over time can transform an acquaintance into a cherished and trusted friend. But there are ways to do it wrong! Most socially anxious people err on the side of sharing too little; but if you're still finding your feet in this area, there's a danger of the pendulum swinging too far in the other direction! Watch out for...

Mistake 1: Your self-disclosures are too much, too soon

- Example: On a first date you tell all the gory details about every last one of your exes, blab all your darkest secrets, share the names you want to give to your future kids, and complain about your foot rash.

The best and most effective self-disclosures are *tiny*.

They fit the stage that the relationship is currently at. To be effective, you only need to disclose a little here, a little there. Take your time and be patient.

It's more like grains filtering through the middle of an hourglass than a devastating avalanche!

You don't have to reveal everything about yourself all at once to be authentic or honest. Pace yourself. Make minor disclosures in the early stages, and save the bigger, heavier stuff for later.

Finally, realize that you don't have to share everything with everyone. You can be selective. Good relationships do grow, but if you're happy with where a relationship is (or they are) then you don't have to *force it* to progress. It's OK to keep some of yourself back.

Mistake 2: Your self-disclosures are lopsided and unbalanced

- Example: You confide in a colleague about some mental health issues you're having. They're polite and listen. You keep telling them more and more... never quite realizing that they haven't told you a single thing about themselves.

There really is a rhythm with self-disclosure. Trust and liking only develops when there is a reciprocal and balanced "call and response" structure.

- You reveal a little
- They see that revelation
- They respond well
- They reveal a little in turn
- You see what they reveal
- You respond well
- You choose to reveal a little more
- And so on!

A useful rule of thumb: Never offer two self-disclosures in a row. Instead, self-disclose, then stop. Wait to see their reaction before you make another disclosure.

Note: There's a difference between responding positively to a disclosure and reciprocating it. People can be attentive and kind and accepting. But what you want to pay attention to is whether they choose to respond with a disclosure of their own.

Is it reciprocated? That's your green light. It's your turn next, and you can escalate, if you want to.

Is it not reciprocated? No problem. You haven't done anything wrong. But don't try to escalate when someone is not responsive. They may be telling you, "This is far enough for me." Acknowledge and respect that. Don't be surprised if they self-disclose later on—we all move at our own pace.

Mistake 3: Your self-disclosures are a burden

- "Don't tell anyone, but I've been skimming off the checking account for years, and management has never noticed…"

There is a fine line between being vulnerable and making unfair and inappropriate emotional demands on people. How can you tell the difference?

A self-disclosure starts to become a burden when it benefits the person making it, but harms the one hearing it, or puts them in a difficult position. Revealing a heavy secret just for your own relief? Not only is it inconsiderate, but it may also backfire—and mean that you don't receive the support you actually need.

Though you're unlikely to make this kind of revelation to a random acquaintance, beware of accidentally going too far with a growing friendship.

Mistake 4: Your self-disclosures are just plain inappropriate

Finally, understand that there are just some things that never need to be said, to anyone, no matter how close to them you may feel. Remember that self-disclosures can't be taken back.

Self-disclosure can be thrilling. It can feel like a little reward—to say something a little unexpected and vulnerable, and to have it well received. But sometimes, this little thrill can mean we forget ourselves—especially if alcohol is involved! You can find yourself happily spilling your guts only to feel mortified later when sense returns.

Avoid mean-spirited gossip. Don't exaggerate or say things that are inaccurate or plain untrue. As a rule, keep something back—you can build plenty of rapport and trust without becoming an over-sharer!

Tip: Don't worry about always making the first move or putting yourself in the spotlight. You can invite other people to self-disclose, too. Even one slightly personal question and answer exchange can significantly increase closeness—remember that it's all about responsiveness and reciprocal trust. Recall Aron and colleagues' "36 questions" and dare to ask something a little out of left field.

"What's something you're feeling excited about lately?"

Tip 2: Is someone already self-disclosing to you? That's your cue—they may want to get closer! Chronic over-sharers and gossips aside, you could be looking at real untapped friendship potential. The ball is in your court, so acknowledge the emotional risk they've already taken, and reciprocate.

Chapter 15: "My Disagreements With People Get Out of Hand."

The unfolding of a new friendship is a beautiful thing—like a dance. One takes a tiny step towards more intimacy, vulnerability, and authenticity, and the other acknowledges and reflects it. Soon, both are more *in sync*, and a connection emerges, one move at a time.

Gradually, we relax a little.

We let more and more of ourselves be seen.

In turn, we may be surprised at the unexpected traits and opinions we find in *them*…

And here's precisely where things can start to go wrong! After a while, increasing comfort and familiarity mean we lower our guards and, well, we stop making quite so much of an effort. In the best way possible, we are no longer on our very best behavior. And that can have unexpected consequences.

- **One side of the healthy relationship coin:** Understanding how to foster rapport and connection, engage well, gradually escalate, build trust, and strengthen your empathy and understanding.
- **But there's another side:** Knowing how to handle minor conflicts, misunderstandings, disagreements, or differences of opinion so they don't

threaten the amazing connection you've built!

Some of us are actually pretty good at making friends. The trouble is preserving that bond once the "honeymoon period" is over and the little cracks start to show. In a way, finding people you like is just part of the task—but the other part is knowing what to do when you discover the parts you *don't* like about one another.

If your friendships tend to take on a boom-and-bust pattern, or if you often bond instantly with new people only to have a dramatic falling out shortly after, then this may be an area of concern for you.

Disagreements and clashes can arise for all sorts of complicated reasons. However, in this chapter, we won't be considering any of them. Instead, we'll look at **the single thing that most often prolongs and extends disagreements: people feeling like they're not being heard.**

It doesn't matter what it's about, or how serious the topic is; communication inevitably breaks down when one or both parties feel like they are no longer being listened to.

That means that one of the best social skills you can learn is how to quickly defuse:

- slight misunderstandings,
- awkwardness,
- little disagreements,

- unexpected disappointments,
- hurt feelings, and
- petty arguments—

before they become full-blown conflicts that threaten the relationship.

Mindless, self-focused, or inconsiderate listening at a delicate time can have people raising their guard and going on the defensive. Within minutes, something very important happens—the Shift.

The Shift = The switch from seeing one another as friends and allies, to seeing one another as enemies and potential threats.

- It's suddenly you vs. them.
- It's no longer a conversation, but a battle, a court room drama, a debate, an interrogation.
- It's not about focusing on them and their perspective (external focus) but on protecting yourself and your perspective (self-focus).

Once this shift has already happened (and it can happen quickly!) then it can be increasingly difficult to reign in the bad feelings and reconnect without blame, anger, or suspicion.

When people feel hurt (regardless of whether you've actually hurt them), they go into survival mode. Their goal is no longer to hear you or collaborate with you. It's to protect themselves from you.

When people feel unheard, they feel invalidated, unimportant, or even disrespected. Their goal is no longer to listen to you, it's to speak louder so that *you* listen to *them*. They may even give up entirely and shut down.

Their defensiveness triggers yours, and yours reinforces theirs.

Though it's always possible to rescue a relationship from a serious conflict, the smarter move is to make sure you never make the Shift in the first place.

How?

The Solution

One of the easiest and yet most effective ways to protect harmony and maintain an open, trusting connection is to make sure people feel heard by **practicing active listening**. Listening well is not just for serious chats and conflict resolution—it's a way to avoid conflicts all together.

As with everything else we've discussed in this book, the trick lies in effectively making a certain shift in attitude.

Active listening is about so, so much more than nodding, smiling, and patiently waiting for the other person to stop talking so that you can speak!

Active listening is really an *attitude* and an *orientation*. It's a way of seeing the other person that, when fully manifested, makes it almost impossible to get into a messy or awkward argument.

The active listening advice you'll find out there will tell you to:

- Nod
- Use encouraging phrases
- Make eye contact
- Use open body language
- Reflect and paraphrase what you hear
- Don't interrupt
- Offer your undivided attention

It's not that this advice is wrong, **but these behaviors do not constitute active listening in themselves. Rather, they are the *external expressions* of active listening.** They may tick the boxes to show that we are listening, but our goal is not just to give a convincing *appearance* of listening actively. Our goal is to actually do it!

If this distinction seems like hair-splitting, try to think back to a time when someone might have been doing all of the above as they listened to you—but somehow you still didn't feel *heard*.

Why? Because truly hearing someone, *truly listening to them*, is not a set of behaviors, but a deeper attitude. A mindset. It's a way of receiving another person and the message they're sharing. It's the essence of communication… and it cannot be faked.

Itzchakov and colleagues (2024, *Journal of Personality and Social Psychology*) find that "[high quality] listening influences depolarization through positivity resonance and nondefensive self-reflection."

In other words, really listening to people is a way to defuse tension, de-escalate arguments, and build real bridges between people's differences. It does this because it makes people feel genuinely seen and heard, which:

- makes them feel safer,
- helps them not to view one another as threats, and
- means they don't make the Shift—

which means there's no need to go to war with one another!

Active listening can transform a minor disagreement into an opportunity for even deeper connection, trust, and understanding.

Were you able to navigate a small quarrel successfully? Then you've found a way to communicate something really special to the other person: "You can trust me. I care about staying connected to you more than I care about being right. I'm always going to be kind and respectful, even when we don't see eye to eye."

If you can embody *that* attitude and that mindset, then your disagreements will never get out of hand!

Let's take a closer look at some practical ways to start embodying the active listening attitude:

- **Drop the need to counterargue.** The impulse to explain or justify yourself, push back, or go on the defensive comes purely from fear. We may even find ourselves arguing just to be contrary. When someone shares something we don't agree with, like, or understand, the temptation is to view it as a mild threat or challenge against which we have to protect ourselves.
  - But here's the secret: You don't!
  - Don't immediately try to figure out what your opinion is and whether you think they are correct, rational, reasonable, or even allowed to have that opinion.
  - Get out of the habit of responding with, "Well, actually..."
  - When you're listening to someone, choose in that moment to *just listen to them.* It's not that you don't matter. It's just not your turn. Shelve your perspective for a moment and look at theirs—in its entirety.
- **Listen to understand, not to respond.** When emotions are running high and there

are polarizing views thrown in the mix (lots of those around today, right?), we can start to unconsciously frame interactions as contests or battles. But this only acts to decrease safety, increase threat, and ramp up conflict. Instead:

- Don't mentally formulate and rehearse a counter-response while they're still speaking. It may sound strange, but try not to think about what you're going to say at all. Just focus on fully and completely hearing their message, in the moment, without considering how it measures up against *yours*.
- Understand that you can always validate and show empathy for a person EVEN IF you don't share, like, or understand their opinion. You might like to mentally separate the two things out: You are having a disagreement, but you still value them and you still value the relationship. This is often framed as: **"It's me and you vs. the problem, never me vs. you."**
- Your first priority is just to *hear one another.* Try to remind yourself that you don't have to convince, persuade, defend, justify, apologize, ask for permission, or grant it. Friction isn't necessarily a disaster, nor is it a cue to desperately try to force agreement.
- Tip: Try pausing for a few moments after people speak. Take the time to digest what

you've heard, instead of barging in with your own contribution.

- **Set aside your ego.** Sometimes, the only thing getting in the way of us being more effective listeners is our own pride. When people share how they feel, we may feel embarrassed, criticized, called out, or like we've been declared deficient in some way. Basically, we take it personally! It's the egocentric bias again, and it only stresses *us* out.
  - Instead, have enough emotional maturity to focus on first hearing, respecting, and validating them. How can you make them feel seen, heard, validated, and respected? It's not that their needs are more important than ours. It's just that acknowledging theirs will make it much easier for them to acknowledge ours!

The next time you feel a conversation going a little sour or you notice that slight feeling of awkwardness arise, pause. Become aware.

Your focus: Reduce feelings of threat.

Your method: Make people feel heard with high-quality listening.

Have they said something kind of rude?

Shared an opinion that has your hackles up?

Made a comment or joke or criticism that feels a little "off"?

Are you feeling... hurt? Offended? Disappointed?

Or perhaps you've just become aware that they feel those things about *you*?

Just stop. Breathe. Be aware that at that very moment you can choose what happens next. You do not have to make the Shift and start viewing them as an enemy or sparring partner. And you can conduct yourself so that they do not see you that way, either.

Be aware of any desire to hit back, argue, or elevate yourself. Be aware of that sinking feeling that makes you want to put up walls or retreat. See all those kneejerk reactions... and watch yourself choose not to engage with them.

Then, take a deep breath and **turn your attention outward.** Genuinely, truly, sincerely and with all your heart, try to understand what they're saying, where they're coming from, and what their perspective is. Give them the benefit of the doubt. Listen generously—assuming the best.

Give them the compassion and consideration you wish others would give to your thoughts and opinions. If you don't quite understand something, ask clarifying questions. Try to understand *why* they're saying what they're saying.

Your goal is never to rank your opinions against theirs, make them think as you do, or protect yourself from them trying to convert you. You're just trying to see into one another's worlds. You're trying to re-establish harmony and connection.

Now let's return to that conventional listening advice from before:

- Nod
- Use encouraging phrases
- Make eye contact
- Use open body language
- Reflect and paraphrase what you hear
- Don't interrupt
- Offer your undivided attention

When you **hold the attitude that the other person is worthy, that you respect them, and that you are genuinely curious about their perspective**, then you will automatically do all of the above.

Chapter 16: "I Don't Have a Big Social Battery."

Could you be a "social Cinderella"?

Maybe you're out at the ball, having an amazing time, but when the clock strikes midnight (or, let's be honest, more like 9:30 p.m.) suddenly your gown turns into rags, your carriage turns back into a pumpkin, and you find yourself beating a hasty retreat.

Your battery's run out and you just have no more to give. Perhaps you're so drained by even the thought of long-haul social gatherings that you find yourself avoiding them completely.

You're not alone!

While the norm is to think of social energy and orientation in terms of *introversion* and *extroversion*, it may be that there are finer, more nuanced distinctions to be made:

- We may feel extroverted and outgoing—but only for short bursts.
- We may feel more introverted when unwell, tired, or stressed out, but more extroverted when relaxed and happy.
- We may be extremely chatty and gregarious with those we know well, but shy with strangers.
- We may be alert, sociable, and high energy in the morning, but ready to retreat to the sofa by 7 p.m.—or vice versa.

- We might be naturally lively and friendly and engaging for extended periods, but then also need extended periods of alone time to recharge.

Basically, we're all different.

Just as we each have different circadian rhythms and individual cycles of rest and productivity, most of us have our own *social rhythms*. It's less about whether we are introverted or extroverted, and more about whether we are adequately supporting our unique social needs and preferences.

The Solution

This may seem almost too simple, but: **If you don't enjoy socializing for long periods, *then don't socialize for long periods.***

If intense hours-long conversations drain you, you don't have to have them.

Indeed, if horse-drawn carriages and ballgowns aren't quite your style, you can opt out of those, too!

The trouble comes when we adopt a kind of all-or-nothing mindset: Either we are hyper-energetic social butterflies who can go all night, *or* we stay cooped up at home in our slippers, asking the pizza delivery guy to just leave it on the doorstep. We (wrongly) tell ourselves there is no in-between.

But there is! Could it be time to revisit some socializing misconceptions that might be keeping you limited?

Misconception 1: Extended social marathons are the gold standard

When you think about it—who says so?

Some people sincerely enjoy all-night benders, lengthy group holidays, and parties that go on and on and on. But it's simply not true that the longer a social gathering, the better.

In fact, research shows that **even brief and low-key interactions with acquaintances can increase well-being and boost your feelings of belonging.** In their paper, "Is efficiency overrated? Minimal social interactions lead to belonging and positive affect",

Sandstrom & Dunn (2014) put it like this:

> *When we buy our daily cup of coffee, sometimes we engage in a social interaction with the barista, and sometimes we are in a rush. Every day we have opportunities to transform potentially impersonal, instrumental exchanges into genuine social interactions, and the happiness literature suggests that we may reap benefits by doing so; in other words, treating a service provider like we would an acquaintance (a weak tie) might make us happier. In the current study, people who had a social interaction with a*

Their research goes on to explain that even micro-interactions like chatting to a barista count as "weak ties" and can fill up our social tank. In other words, you can feel significant feelings of warmth and connection *without* it having to take hours and hours of time. You can get that boost of belonging without fatigue and social burnout.

Tip: Instead of thinking in terms of *length* of social event, be more interested in their *number* and *quality*. It may be that for you, three 10-minute bursts of lighthearted chit-chat spread throughout the day is *more* beneficial than a single three-hour hangout that leaves you feeling grumpy and depleted afterwards.

Does a proposed social event look kind of grueling? See if you can find a middle ground and not attend the whole thing. Leave a little earlier or arrive a little later, or find a different way to contribute. Most people would rather you came for a little while than not at all!

Misconception 2: Socializing has to be deep and meaningful to be worthwhile

A related socializing myth is the idea that only those deep and meaningful interactions with very close friends "count." Superficial conversation with randoms? Just not as important.

Introverts can sometimes complain that they hardly ever "click" with people, and that nobody understands them. While this may be true, it's also possible that they have slightly unrealistic expectations about just how much they have to like someone to derive value from their company.

Not everyone in your social network has to be a super close friend. In fact, **those of us with more modest social batteries may actually benefit from lighter, shorter, and less intense interactions.** In a way, a superficial chat with a barista is great precisely because it's superficial—it's warm and friendly, but you don't have to think too hard about it, and it's all over in two minutes.

Lighter interactions allow you to shine, but in a low stake, time-limited way. You get to connect, but without force or exhaustion. And you can bail without penalty!

Tip: Work on those weak ties. Consider your work, hobbies, and everyday activities and think of creative ways to connect with others via these channels. Get to know your neighbors or people in your community and engage around time-limited activities that keep interactions friendly but light and fast-moving.

- Make a point to share a few words with various colleagues at work during lunch time, or chat to random people at the dog park. Keep it light. Take the pressure off.

Misconception 3: Socializing has to look a particular way to be valid

Maybe we can blame certain popular TV shows for teaching generations of us to expect friendship to look a certain way. Realistically? A big, tightly knit friend group that does everything together may be more fiction than fact.

Beyond the TV screen, **a "healthy social life" can mean different things to different people.** The way that you engage optimally with your social world will be completely unique to you. There's no point suffering from social life FOMO because you assume that everyone else out there is doing it right and you're doing it wrong.

Instead, figure out what *your* right looks like.

- **An enormous friend group is actually not the norm.** A study at the Pew Research Center (2024) claimed that for Americans, the average number of close friends is 1 to 5, and that most people are fairly satisfied with this. That means that even if you only have one or two friends, you're not failing—you're perfectly average.
- **Your social needs change over time.** Your social life will depend on many factors:

your age, gender, life stage, occupation, culture, income level, whether you're partnered or have kids, your politics and religion, your health status, and how much free time you have, just to name a few! What works when you're a 35-year-old married dad of two may not be what worked when you were in high school.

- **It doesn't have to look like a *Friends* episode.** Get creative! There are as many ways to connect with people as there are people—what would you most enjoy?
  o Find interest groups and clubs online if local opportunities are lacking.
  o Seek out an old-fashioned pen-pal.
  o Join a band.
  o Volunteer at the old folks' home or animal shelter.
  o Sign up for home exchange holidays.
  o Join a support group.
  o Attend a cooking or dancing class.
  o Go to big concerts or festivals alone.
  o Use social media to find those with shared interests.
  o Check out meetup.com or your local equivalent.
  → Some of these tips may work, and some won't. All that matters is that you experiment and find out what works *for you.*

Chapter 17: "My Long-Distance Friendships Fade."

Although we're constantly told that the world is now a hyperconnected place, and that friends halfway around the world are now magically available with the push of a button, the truth is that long-distance relationships are as hard now as they ever were.

There's no way around it: When people move further apart, friendships change. There are fewer face-to-face interactions and greatly reduced opportunities for human touch—which is a subtle but powerful modulator for intimacy, even in platonic relationships.

Even close and well-meaning friends can find that going long-distance just feels... different. As people relocate or move through their various life transitions, certain friendships may quietly take a back seat or be moved down the priority list...

The unfortunate truth is that **unless there is a mutual attempt to maintain that relationship, it will fade and fizzle.**

The Solution

Long-distance relationships require more deliberate and conscious effort than those that can fall back on proximity and habit.

When you inhabit the same social world as someone else, you also share a host of triggers, cues, and prompts with them, and these can do much of the heavy lifting of bringing you and the other person together.

But when people physically move away from one another, they no longer inhabit the same social world in quite the same way. They are no longer exposed to the same triggers, cues, or prompts that would automatically push them together. In fact, the only way they *will* ever find themselves in one another's orbits is if they intentionally plan for it!

Long-distance friendship *can* work, but they often need to be consciously transitioned into **a new kind of relationship entirely—one built not on chance but on choice.**

What will help relationships stay strong even in the face of distance?

- **Strategic communication.** It may feel unnatural at first, especially if your previous friendship was more spontaneous, but it's important to commit to a predictable "check in" schedule that has you reaching out in consistent ways, across a range of different channels, i.e. video call, phone call, email, text message, and specially organized in-person meetings.
  - Moderate your expectations. You may feel that you should be more frequently in touch, but be patient as your friendship finds its new rhythm. One study found that even a

single annual check-in can keep a connection alive and maintain a feeling of support (Finchum, 2005).

- o Don't wait for things to happen spontaneously—they likely won't. Instead, schedule check-ins every month, diarize birthdays and other important dates, and make getting in touch a new, non-negotiable habit.
- o Tip: Pick one channel + one time (the first Sunday of the month, phone call, etc.), and make it automatic.

- **Find ways to share experiences.** When people are not in sync socially in ordinary, everyday ways, they can find they have little to talk about when they do chat. The friendship can devolve into a tedious series of obligatory conversations and the feeling that here is just way too much to "catch up" on each time. Soon, the awkwardness of not feeling connected to one another's worlds can lead to just avoiding contact altogether.

- o Where possible, commit to in-person visits, even if very infrequent. Make memories by sharing new experiences and moments together—things you can both look back fondly on.
- o Where not possible, get creative: Virtually watch the same movie together, read the same book, or keep it casual and do chores and activities while connected digitally. You'll get the sense that you're still doing

things together, and there will always be something current to talk about.

- o Your goal is to continue to find ways to maintain a *shared identity*, and a *shared history* with one another. Lean into in-jokes and memories that only you two share. Reminisce together or have fun planning new experiences… and looking forward to them together.

- **Be intentional with tech.** The irony of ubiquitous communication tech is that it can make us *less* likely to reach out. Being frequently interrupted with low-effort memes, single word texts, or social media likes does not increase connection or intimacy—but it can create overwhelm and social burnout.

- o Quality over quantity. It may take some trial and error, but find a communication medium, interaction length, and frequency that feels right for both sides. Just being aware of one another won't cut it—you'll need some quality time mixed in, too!

- **Be more obvious**. Is someone physically present in your world? Do they keep accepting your invites and choosing to be around you whenever they can? That tells you that they probably like you and care about you. But with long-distance friendships, this kind of feedback is absent. You may need to deliberately *say* that you care… and more often than you think.

- o Remember important events like birthdays and always check in over Christmas, New Years, or any other holiday relevant to them. Diarize these dates, set up reminders, and consider routinely setting aside money and time for gifts and celebrations.
- o Be considerate. Show an interest in their lives, especially those parts that no longer overlap with yours. It's more important than ever to pay attention to little details you're told. What's on their radar at the moment? What's the weather like where they are?
- o Verbally express that you care, that they matter to you, and that you value their friendship. Send thoughtful letters in the mail, or little voice notes "just because." These emotional signals and reassurances matter—regardless of their content. Getting in touch just to offload about life is unlikely to have the same effect!

But... What If They Never Reciprocate?

Sadly, it can happen.

Maintaining long-distance friendships requires a special touch. But perhaps it also requires flexibility, compassion, and a willingness to manage expectations.

- When friends move, things *will* change—that is unavoidable.

- People's lives go through busy periods, rough patches, complications, and tricky transitions.
- It's normal for friendships of all kinds to ebb and flow, and temporarily not hearing from someone might not mean that anything is wrong.

Things change. What matters is the intentional effort to protect the connection, despite those changes.

It's natural to ask, then: What if the other person just… doesn't want to make the effort?

Today, it's fashionable to suggest that we all "go no contact" with toxic people, cut them from our lives and get ruthless with those relationships that no longer spark joy. This all-or-nothing approach may "work"—but the cost could be isolation and resentment.

On the other hand, nothing can feel lonelier than the creeping sense that your friendships only exist because you're constantly propping them up.

What to do?

Unfortunately, there are no easy rules. Humans are complicated and messy, and getting involved with them is going to be complicated and messy, too! To find a little more clarity, ask yourself the following questions:

- Is this relationship really fading, or is it just changing into something else?
- Is the distance I'm noticing due to their lack of interest, or is it due to circumstances?
- Am I trying to control or take responsibility for this friendship more than I should?
- Without it being anyone's fault, might this friendship have run its course?

Sociologist Gerald Mollenhorst published a study in 2009 explaining the phenomenon of "friendship churn"—the observation that an average person will lose roughly half of their friend group every seven years. Mollenhorst offers some suggestions for why this happens, but it may come down to the simple fact that over the course of seven years, things change.

People move.

They change jobs.

They start dating or break up or marry or divorce or have kids or experience a bereavement.

The good news is that if a friendship lasts longer than seven years, it's statistically more likely to stick around for life. The idea is that if a pair can survive seven years of ups and downs, then it can survive *anything*, and the resulting loyalty and trust strengthen that bond to unbreakable.

But what about the 50% of relationships that *don't* survive the seven-year churn?

These friendships may be good, but they may also be based primarily on *proximity* and *convenience.* That's not necessarily a problem. However, it does mean that when circumstances change, so does the friendship.

With Mollenhorst's observations taken into account, let's add a few more reflection questions:

- Is this friendship based mostly on shared circumstances, convenience, and proximity? Is it changing now because those circumstances are changing?
- Has this friendship survived change before?
- Has this friendship actually changed, or is it that we as people have changed?

Losing friends over the course of life does not mean that you—or they—are doing anything wrong. Some people come into our lives and stay there forever; others don't. If someone is not reciprocating effort to maintain a friendship, it may simply signal that the friendship has reached its natural lifespan. And that's OK.

Chapter 18: "Approaching Strangers Is So Uncomfortable."

Picture this. You're out walking in your town, running errands, when someone approaches you, smiles and asks in a friendly way, "I'm sorry, is the train station further along down this road? Or is it in the next street over?"

Just pause right now and imagine how you would feel if a stranger approached you out of the blue like this.

Chances are, you wouldn't feel annoyed, afraid, or confused. In fact, maybe you'd kind of *like* it and enjoy getting the chance to help someone out, even if only in a small way.

You know where this is going. We typically don't find it uncomfortable when strangers approach us, so why is it so different when the roles are reversed?

Perhaps one day social scientists will identify another cognitive bias that will fully explain this weird social quirk, but for now we can assure ourselves that, rationally, **people are, on average, unlikely to be less receptive to being approached than we ourselves are**.

Of course, you can know something rationally, without actually *believing* it. That's why the only way around this particular social obstacle is to give yourself evidence—experiential evidence—

that approaching strangers is *not* the unbearable and impossible task it may at first seem.

What's more, you need to give yourself experiential evidence that even if someone *doesn't* respond positively, it actually doesn't matter—you are able to recover, move on, and not let it affect you in the slightest.

The Solution

The gulf that separates *stranger* from *friend* can seem enormous and unbroachable.

If you've struggled socially, just saying "Hi" to someone can feel as momentous as mankind's first step on the moon... except maybe a little harder to achieve.

The truth, however, is that **anxiety makes us imagine a terrifying wall that isn't really there.** We can't bear approaching people "cold" because we imagine it'll be awkward, uncomfortable... a disaster we won't recover from.

In reality, approaching a stranger is only dangerous if we believe it is and we are already anxious.

To prove this to yourself, one amazing strategy is to **employ a series of deliberate behavioral experiments.** Your goal is not to gather data about how other people behave (although you'll get this anyway, and it may surprise you!). Instead, the idea is to gently provide real-world counterevidence *for yourself* disproving that approaching people is unpleasant, awkward, uncomfortable, or outright scary.

Here's a suggested plan for how to conduct such an experiment, although you can modify according to your own goals.

Step 1: Carefully examine and record your expectations

Those with high rejection sensitivity have distorted internal models that lead them to expect to be socially rejected far more than they actually are. Some research (Powers et. al., 2014) suggests that people with rejection sensitivity actually show increased activity in the area of the brain associated with reward mechanisms and "mentalizing" about others.

So, what does it mean to *mentalize*?

The authors explain, "As a social species, humans are acutely aware of cues that signal *inclusionary status*." They go on to explain that when people await social feedback, their brains work hard to anticipate possible social cues, interpret them, and make a best guess about people's intentions, and whether they will accept us or not.

In people sensitive to rejection, this process is overactive. Our own anxiety causes us to misperceive and misinterpret social cues, allowing us to come to faulty conclusions.

Let's break this down:

- Rejection sensitivity makes you anxious (afraid that you'll be rejected).
- This anxiety makes you expect rejection.
- This heightened neural response actually makes you more likely to perceive rejection where there isn't any.

In other words, it's a confirmation bias—a kind of misperception that reinforces itself.

Rejection sensitivity can start with your expectations of how others will respond. But in truth, these are not expectations so much as self-fulfilling prophecies and foregone conclusions. **When you have primed yourself to perceive rejection, you're more likely to read a completely neutral or ambiguous reaction as a negative, rejecting one.**

This is why the first step is to start with your *anxious expectations of rejection* and dismantle them piece by piece.

Start with a program of low stakes, daily micro-interactions, like chatting to the barista, asking where the train station is, or telling someone you like their dog. These are not really "approaches" at all. Instead, think of them as practice, data-gathering, or experiments.

The goal: Aim to approach a complete stranger at least once a day.

If you like, you can increase this frequency, but once a day is a great start.

What counts as an approach? Just talk to people—ask them the time, ask for directions, or make a random comment about the weather or whatever.

That's it.

These interactions are light, easy, and at most a few seconds long.

Before you begin, though, get a notebook and carefully record your expectations.

Be precise about exactly what you assume will happen. Remember to make predictions only about those things you can actually observe, like other people's behaviors, not their feelings (remember you are not a mindreader!).

For example:

- I predict that 80% of people will ignore me.
- I expect that afterwards I will feel really awkward and humiliated.
- I guess that people will be curt and won't choose to engage much with me if I ask them a question.

Once you've written down some of your expectations, congratulations! These are now testable *hypotheses*. Let's move on.

Step 2: Conduct the experiment, record the results

It may feel very, *very* difficult to get stated, but remind yourself that the first one is the hardest it will ever be!

You can set your own rules and requirements (for example, not asking the same question two days in a row) but don't let yourself off too easily.

You might...

- Say something friendly to a cashier
- Ask a random person in the queue how much a ticket costs
- Make a causal remark to someone at the bus stop
- Ask someone what time it is

As you progress, you might like to challenge yourself to say more or be a little bolder:

- Give someone a sincere (and appropriate) compliment
- Ask for more substantial help, for example guiding your car into a tight parking space
- Ask someone's opinion on a pair of shoes you're trying on in a shoe store
- Crack a joke

Aim for one stranger approach daily, for at least a month.

It may sound like a lot, but something magical can start to happen as the days turn into weeks:

The sting of anticipated rejection never quite comes and, when it does, you may be surprised to see that you can handle it far better than you guessed.

Let's be real—some people out there are just plain rude. But the more data you gather, the more clearly you can see these encounters in a broader context. Yes, an encounter with a rude person may make you feel discouraged, but after a more positive encounter the very next day, it doesn't seem to matter quite as much.

Keep challenging yourself to do one a day, and don't get discouraged. Don't let a single encounter define your feelings about *all* people, *all* the time. Keep going.

After every encounter, make a quick record, for example:

- Sept 19th : Smiled and said "wow, nice dinosaur boots" to the toddler in the line at the pharmacy. He smiled back. Felt pretty good.
- Sept 20th : Asked a woman at the mall if she knew whether there was a Dunkin' Donuts nearby. She shrugged and said she wasn't sure. Was a bit nerve-wracking, but then... nothing happened. I felt fine.

Step 3: Analyze your data, make conclusions

After a month, you should have some good data to analyze.

Gather your records and ask yourself some questions to help you understand what you're looking at:

- **What percentage of people actually rejected you?** Importantly, realize that rejection sensitivity may push you to read ambiguous or neutral stimuli as negative. So ask if there was any *objective, observable evidence* that people *actually* rejected you.
  - For example, the woman in the mall might have shrugged and said, "I dunno" but this isn't *rejection*—it's just a neutral response. Her rejection of you (and the fear it inspires) is actually just in your head.
- **Were your predictions accurate?** Go back to what you guessed might happen and compare it to what actually happened. Can you see any distortions or exaggerations? For example, did anyone respond far more *positively* than you predicted? Did as many people respond negatively as you expected?
  - For example, you might have guessed that 80% of people would ignore a question or comment. But don't take your word for it— look at the data. You may see, for example, that only 2% of all your approaches went this way.
- **How did your experience change over time?** The first few approaches might have felt excruciating... but did this apprehension last? Maybe by the end of the month, approaching strangers felt like no big deal.

Boring, even. That's good news! It means that you have thoroughly de-bunked your own cognitive biases and proven to yourself that approaching others socially is not a problem—and it can even be fun.

- How did you cope with less positive responses or reactions? What happened afterwards? What have you learned about yourself over the course of the last month?

A caveat: If rejection sensitivity is an issue for you, be aware that your brain may be constantly working overtime to look for proof that supports the conclusions it's already come to—whether they're true or not, and whether there is proof or not!

To counter this, **focus on behaviors, not your interpretations and guesses about people's behaviors.** You need to consistently ask yourself: "Am I trying to mindread? Am I making an assumption or guess, or can I actually observe an objective rejection behavior?"

Pay attention to your thoughts.

- **NO:** "He thinks I'm rude for bothering him..." (Does he? Did he say so? If not, you're trying to mindread. Maybe he thought you were rude, maybe he didn't. Unless you develop psychic superpowers, you just don't have access to that information).
- **YES:** "He answered my question quickly and then ran off in a hurry." (No rejection here.

All you can conclude Is that he was in a hurry for some reason.)

Unfortunately, **prolonged and embedded beliefs around rejection can sometimes cause us to act in ways that actually elicit rejection behaviors from others.** We may not even realize we're doing it, but we may unconsciously adopt behaviors and attitudes that align with our own self-concept as, basically, rejectable people (Ayduk, 2014). For example:

- We may act in defensive, withdrawn, or guarded ways that make it hard for other people to engage with us.
- We dress or present in ways that essentially sends the message, "Don't come too close."
- We may even go on the offensive because, in a strange way, we take the other person's rejection of us as a given and pre-emptively respond to that… even though it hasn't happened yet.

We've already seen that small, low stakes daily social interactions can deliver outsized benefits for our social wellbeing and overall feeling of connectedness (Sandstrom & Dunn, 2014). Daily micro-interactions like these can feel incredibly grounding, making you feel connected and as though you belong to your social landscape.

When you deliberately conduct behavioral experiments to approach strangers in a controlled and deliberate way, you also take steps to dismantle limiting beliefs about rejection—beliefs that are keeping you from experiencing that everyday sense of connection and belonging.

One final tip: **Be aware of gender dynamics**. For obvious reasons, women may be more prone to rejecting men they feel are approaching with ulterior motives, and men in turn may approach interactions with heightened expectations of rejection. A good idea is just to remove the gender element entirely at first, and approach only same-sex strangers in a platonic way.

Be warm, friendly, and appropriate.

Build up slowly.

Remember that you are not approaching people in order to extract any particular response from them. It's not even really about them. It's about *you*. Get used to making approaches, get comfortable with speaking up, and learn what it feels like to see other people as no big deal.

You'll set up a self-fulfilling prophecy, but in the other direction.

Remember: Rejection sensitivity is worsened by avoidance, but soothed by gradual exposure that helps you build tolerance in tiny, easy-to-manage ways.

Chapter 19: "I've Been Hurt Before. I Won't Open Up Again."

You might have read the previous section with some suspicion. The only reason you expect rejection, you think, is because you actually *have* been rejected in the past. Perhaps quite cruelly, and perhaps more than once.

This wasn't a cognitive distortion and it wasn't a self-fulfilling prophecy. This was you opening up and trusting someone... and then being mistreated.

Maybe you shared a secret and someone failed to treat it with tact and respect. Maybe you revealed a weakness and were mocked for it. Maybe you took the risk of being vulnerable with someone, only to have them use it against you later.

Some of us may be carrying very specific memories of past trauma (like a breakup or betrayal), while others can't point to any particular episode—it's more like life in general has taught them to guard their hearts and never give anyone the chance to hurt them.

Does this sound like you?

- You may be perfectly friendly and engaging on the surface, but somehow people sense there is a part of yourself that you're always holding back.

- You may be talented, capable, self-reliant, and independent, but others see you as aloof, proud, and even judgmental.
- You feel like you are content with the psychological reserves you've built up for yourself, and that you like not needing other people that much.
- You feel lonely sometimes and find it hard to connect with people. It's like you're an alien, or like everyone else got the memo except you.

If any of this resonates, it may be a sign that your biggest obstacle to social connection is a wound from the past.

These old relational injuries may have even come from earliest childhood, where our parents were the first to teach us whether the world and the people in it were fundamentally trustworthy... or not.

Responding to hurt by withdrawing is a perfectly logical response. Not everyone *is* safe or deserving of our trust, openness, and vulnerability... and recognizing that takes courage.

However, there are costs to withdrawing and choosing to be less involved with humanity. The coping mechanisms that might have kept us safe in the past can keep us limited and shut down in the present.

If connection and intimacy are a theme park, then trust and vulnerability are the entrance fee.

Boundaries are important, but what matters is how those boundaries are functioning. We need to ask ourselves:

- Is this barrier I've put up *protecting* me?
- Or is it *keeping me apart* from the people I might benefit from contact with?

Putting up a barrier can keep us safe, but it can also keep us anonymous, unable to experience others, or have them experience us.

Safe, yes, but lonely!

The Solution

Controlled self-disclosure rebuilds trust.

We've already seen that trust is a thing that grows slowly, step by step, like a seedling.

Trust that has been broken is like cutting down a tree. The old tree is gone; *if* it grows again (note the *if*, not *when*), it will have to start again from the beginning, as a seedling.

When your trust has been broken, or when it feels like you've exposed yourself only to get hurt, the understandable response is to quickly shut down again, retreat, and put up barriers. But then what?

It can be hard to recalibrate and re-discover what's normal.

Luckily, there has been plenty of fascinating research investigating how people actually form healthy relationships, and how trust, intimacy, vulnerability, and gradual self-disclosure all work together.

Let's take a look.

In 1973, Altman and Taylor proposed their *Social Penetration Theory*, which describes how intimacy develops over time: through gradual self-disclosure. However, it does so across two dimensions:

- Depth
- Breadth

When you're first getting to know someone, your self-disclosures will be around topics of wide breadth, but low depth.

You'll talk about weather, popular TV shows, food, and what you did over the weekend.

With time, as you build trust and get to know one another, you may narrow the breadth to more selected topics, but go deeper into those topics.

You'll talk more about your personal opinions, your preferences, your life goals and struggles, your past, and all the things that make you the person you are.

In time, you go even deeper. You may share very private information, your more raw emotions, or things that very few people know about.

For some of us, making the leap from shallow to deep can feel like a minefield. But the process is actually quite sequential, logical, and perfectly predictable. In fact, it follows a handful of simple rules:

- **Relationships move from superficial to intimate** via degrees of reciprocal, gradual self-disclosure.
- **Self-disclosure builds trust** because it reduces uncertainty, but the reciprocity itself also signals a willingness to invest in the relationship and "play fair."
- **Healthy self-disclosure is reciprocal and balanced.** One person shares, then the other does. Self-disclosure creates intimacy, but so does this deliberate turn-taking, which creates an atmosphere of fairness, predictability, and safety.
- **Finally, relationships can "de-penetrate",** meaning trust can be broken and intimacy lost. When relationship costs officially outweigh rewards, the result is a reduction in both breadth and depth.

Self-disclosure and trust are in constant interplay. But as you can see, trust is not just about what you do—it's also about how they respond to what you do.

Important: When we've been hurt, our risk perception can go a little haywire. It can seem like opening up to another person is all cost and no reward. We might even come to feel that trust in general is a foolish thing to do... why expose ourselves to others and take the risk?

However, this attitude comes from a fundamental misunderstanding about how trust actually develops in relationships. Being vulnerable is never meant to be compromising, unsafe, or shouldered by one party alone; **it's something you do together**.

It's a shared risk.

It's a mutual deepening.

If you like, think of it as a friendly hostage situation—you never need to put yourself in a situation that the other person isn't also willing to be in!

Trust is both a precondition and an outcome. It's a catch-22: you need some baseline trust to self-disclose, but self-disclosure itself increases trust. One tiny reinforcing gesture at a time, you create a positive feedback loop, and the seedling grows.

Building trust is not about merely deciding you're going to trust someone. It's not something anyone is entitled to by default.

Rather, trust is a consequence. It's a natural result of mutual, reciprocal vulnerability.

- **Start small and safe**. Whether you're building trust for the first time or re-establishing it after a rupture, take your time and make sure that you're moving at a pace that is comfortable for you. Begin with less risky disclosures (remember that in the beginning, *more breadth* and *less depth* are appropriate) and don't rush or jump ahead. Gradually move into more personal revelations, one finely calibrated step at a time.

- **Keep it reciprocal**. Sometimes people don't have "trust issues" at all—they're just correctly responding to an imbalance in a relationship. Pay close attention to the give-and-take of self-disclosure and keep vulnerability levels roughly equal. This will strengthen trust.

- **Be aware of responsiveness.** Sharing can be risky; if self-disclosures are met with understanding, validation, and acceptance, then trust grows; if they are ignored, judged, or dismissed, people can retreat or shut down. Be aware not only of what people do with your self-disclosures, take care how you receive theirs.

- **Work on your self-esteem.** Some studies show that higher self-esteem is correlated with greater readiness to be vulnerable with others (McCarthy et. al., 2017). Why? Presumably because confident, self-assured people naturally anticipate positive responses. When you share with others, try to remind yourself of your own non-negotiable, unconditional worth. The more secure and self-accepting you are, the easier you'll find it to be yourself with other people.

- **Timing and context matter**. What stage of the relationship are you in? What kind of relationship is it? What's the history and how does that impact what's going on now? All of these things will influence how much and how fast you can build trust. Bear in mind that your goal is not to trust everyone completely, but rather to find a trust level that makes sense in context.

- **You can de-escalate if you want to.** Just because someone has had your trust at some point in the past doesn't mean that they are entitled to it forever. Trust is a joint creation. You don' have to self-disclose and be vulnerable just because the other person is!

Re-Evaluate Your Boundaries

Sometimes, people's boundaries can vacillate between too rigid *and* too porous:

Scenario 1: You're a people-pleaser who says yes to every request and allows people to walk all over you while you quietly seethe with resentment. Then one day, fed up with being taken for granted, you explode at someone, burn bridges, and say a few choice words you quickly regret.

→ Your boundaries were too permeable, but you overcorrected and made them too rigid as a result.

Scenario 2: You may have been overly cautious and emotionally guarded in the past, keeping people at arm's length, unwilling to let anyone into your fortress. And you feel lonely as a result. But one day, desperately longing for real contact, you get a little tipsy and say way, way more than you intended to a new acquaintance, baring your soul and blurting out a few embarrassing secrets.

→ Your boundaries were too rigid, but you overcorrected and made them too porous as a result!

Both of these cases are really a reflection of the same problem: a lack of skill and familiarity with the trust and vulnerability "rules."

Learning to master the art of intimacy means learning to proactively regulate risk and exposure. As you fine-tune these skills, keep pausing to check in with yourself:

- Keep self-disclosures in order: shallow before deep, general before specific.
- Keep self-disclosures small and take it slow, one step at a time.
- Keep self-disclosures reciprocal and balanced. Not balanced? It's OK to pause or even backtrack.
- Keep self-disclosures in line with context and friendship stage.

Finally, remember that **we find out whether we can trust people by trusting them.**

Chapter 20: "I Can't Find My People."

The final social obstacle we will explore is in truth a formidable one. We may say, "I never meet anyone," but what we really mean is, "I never meet anyone *I really like.*"

People can tell you to join a book club or volunteer at the soup kitchen all they like, but deep down you may feel doubtful that this is where you'll meet your tribe. Your people. The friends that really *get* you.

This problem is not insignificant. We might know that getting out there and socializing is important, but spending time with people who don't feel like they're on our wavelength can paradoxically make us feel lonelier than ever.

When you spend time with people you don't quite feel aligned with, you can start to question your own beliefs and attitudes. Are you the weird one out? Should you be changing yourself?

Over time, these feelings of misalignment can start to actually feel like disagreement—and that decreases liking and attraction over time.

The similarity-attraction hypothesis explains that the desire to hang around people who are like us is a natural and ubiquitous one. Basically, **people like people who are like them**. If they are similar in:

- interests,

- values,
- traits,
- attitudes,
- personality,
- demographics, or
- background—

birds of a feather do flock together! Humans form stronger, more enjoyable relationships with people who are like themselves. The idea is that the experience of having our opinions, views, or perceptions contradicted by those quite different from us feels uncomfortable. It's hard to like people under those circumstances.

When people think and feel in ways congruent with our own, however, it creates a feeling of harmony and ease—which can easily be interpretated as liking.

Here's the kicker though: It may not actually be similarity that drives interpersonal attraction, but *perceived* similarity. What makes us like one another is the perception of ease and harmony—whether we really are similar to the other person or not!

Enter an interesting 2008 study by Montoya et. al., which concluded that people are attracted to those they *believe* are similar to them. This "cognitive consistency" validates and confirms their own beliefs and attitudes, which feels like attraction.

This has amazing implications, one of which is this: **Maybe there are no "tribes."**

What if there *isn't* some fabulous group out there filled with only the kinds of people you would most get on with?

What if what really matters is our beliefs and perceptions about other people, and whether they are like us or not?

Consider, for example, how teenagers often group and organize themselves: by fashion choice, music taste, or participation in some subculture.

But is it really true that people who like the same things are similar to one another? And does it follow that they will like one another more? Is it really the case that sharing the same demographics or cultural background means you are more likely to establish a close friendship?

The more you think about it, the less it makes sense.

It's Really About Core Values

Perhaps when we perceive similarity between ourselves and another person, what we are really doing is scanning for **external markers of internal core values** that we may share with them.

It's not enough to just overlap with people in terms of their superficial interests or traits. What matters is deeper compatibility.

The trouble is that random social encounters alone will seldom lead to feelings of real compatibility. Attending general social groups and meetups will simply expose you to the widest possible cross-section of people—those with any number of traits and perspectives.

You *might* meet your next best friend at the gym or coffee shop, but chances are you'll just meet a random member of the public who has little in common with you.

On the other hand, joining interest-based groups or those centered around superficial demographics may also backfire. You could sign up to a local dog-walking group, join a single parents' club, or enroll in a networking group for people in your field. But does that *really* mean that the people you encounter will be part of "your tribe"?

Here's a better strategy: Deliberately seek out *values-based* groups.

Of course, you can never tell exactly who you'll click with, but the better your filters and the finer your selection criteria, the more likely it is that you'll find people who are really like you *on a core level*. And that means easier, more enjoyable, and more natural friendships.

Forcing connections where they don't exist can be demoralizing, and hunting for kindred folk in a crowd of millions can be exhausting. Instead, ask yourself:

"What are my values? Deep down, what kind of person am I?"

Values-based groups are those that comfortably align with your answer to that question.

Go beyond your interest and hobbies, and ask *why* you like those things. Go deeper than your personality traits, history, and demographics, and ask about those things that make you *you*. The better you understand yourself, the more effectively you will be able to locate others like you in the world.

Think about:

- Your perspective and worldview
- Your politics
- Your religious orientation
- Your lifestyle and goals
- Your skills, aptitudes, and education
- Your history

The best way to connect with people who are living the kind of life that makes sense to you is to actually live that life yourself. It's old advice but good advice: You are more likely to meet compatible people when you're already out there and engaging with those parts of the world that speak to your values. Birds of a feather do flock together, so find out where the flock is! This may not always be obvious. Consider:

Activism and volunteering. One great way to expose yourself to people with compatible world views is to engage in activities explicitly centered around values.

- Attending a march, charity fundraiser, community event, or even a public talk or debate can bring you closer to people who think the way you think.

Connect on the spiritual or philosophical level. Get curious about any local churches, temples, or centers that might cater to kindred souls. Investigate whether universities or colleges around you offer free talks or courses, or check community notice boards for workshops, meet-and-greets and other events.

- Whether it's meditation, a Q and A session, or a talk by an author, guru, or minister, you'll not only increase your chance of finding like-minded folk, but the stage will already be set for deeper and more interesting conversation.

Seek out expats, outsiders, and loners. It's counterintuitive, but occasionally the thing that binds people most closely together is the fact that they don't fit anywhere else! If you're new in town, in a complicated life transition or have just lost your friendship group in a breakup, try looking specifically for groups that frame themselves as a home for social misfits.

- Expat communities, support groups, and even those centered around neurodiversity or alternative lifestyles may be where your next potential friend is hiding out.

Similarity Isn't Everything

While of course there is some evidence that people like those who are like them, there's also evidence that people simply like those who they spend the most time with (Newcombe, 1956).

When you like someone, you choose to hang out with them more. But the opposite may also be true: The more you hang out with them, the more liking you develop for one another.

In other words, **similarity matters, but so do proximity and familiarity.**

Good friendships aren't always *discovered*—often, they're *created*.

We can all hold unrealistic expectations about what the ideal friend should look like. We might imagine that our best possible friend is, essentially, a copy of ourselves. But is that really true?

If you've already met someone eerily similar to yourself, you'll already know that this doesn't automatically imply a good relationship!

So, we can add another important factor—
complementarity.

Those who are identical and agree on everything? They have nothing to talk about.

On the other hand, some of the most fun and interesting conversations are those where people are pleasantly different—and they're enjoying the process of learning about that difference.

Your "tribe", then, may not be composed of people who are like you at all, but rather people who are *different enough from you for it to be interesting, fun, and generative.*

- You might not agree with someone's politics but love their fashion sense.
- You might not understand someone's religious beliefs, but you bond over books and music.
- You might have completely different lifestyles and pace of living, but connect over a shared history and cultural identity.

People are multidimensional.

There are helpful ways to sort and organize them, but in reality, there are no categories of people—just people. Each one totally unique.

If your hurdle is the feeling that you will never find your people, it might be worth shifting perspective and thinking instead in terms of relationship functionality. Not about who people are, but about the kind of connection you can make with them.

For example, your friend group might include:

- One friend with whom you have no intellectual connection, but you love doing activities together, like sports, DIY, and hiking. They're who you go to when you have a practical problem.
- The bond you share with another friend is all about the fact that you experienced similar traumas in the past. You understand one another on that level. They're not a "fun" friend—but you trust them with your life.
- A third friend completely lacks this emotional connection, but you have fantastic in-depth conversations about history, politics, life, the universe, and everything. You see them once a month or so.
- A fourth friend is a good two decades older than you, and you both enjoy the totally different perspectives you bring to one another. Plus, you love the same bands and go to concerts together once a year.

Basically? **Similarity is overrated**. When you let go of similarity as a requirement for admission into your tribe, the world opens up in new and exciting ways. Then it doesn't matter, for example, that someone has different political views, is a different age, or isn't what you'd normally consider "your type."

With an open mind and a genuine spirit of curiosity, you bond over something deeper—complementarity, connection, and core values.

Bonus: Magic Phrases and the Science of Good Vibes

In this final section, we'll be taking a look at a few short phrases and expressions that are so predictable in their positive effect on others, they could almost be called magical. When you're in the middle of a conversation, things can move pretty quickly. If you're still working on your social skills and gradually improving your conversational capacities, it can be a little too quick!

You can find yourself floundering about exactly what you should say, moment by moment.

These short phrases will come to your rescue. It's easy. Get familiar with a few of them so that they become practically automatic. **The idea is to memorize these phrases—or phrases very much like them—and keep them in your communication inventory.** That way, you'll always have something to whip out no matter how fast the conversation moves, or where it goes.

A great side effect of this? You'll feel calmer and more confident… and paradoxically won't need to depend on these phrases quite so much!

Let's dive in.

What is the purpose of a "magical phrase"?

That's simple: to create feelings of goodness and positivity.

Very simply, a magical phrase:

- Makes the other person feel good
- Makes the conversation feel good
- Makes you look good

These magical phrases are pretty simple to use, but a few caveats:

- **A little goes a long way**. Think of these magical phrases as salt and pepper—*a little* sprinkled over the top will greatly improve a conversation. Aim for a maximum of one to three phrases per conversation. The shorter and less intimate the conversation, the fewer you'll need.
- **Be sincere**. These phrases really are magical, but they can't bend reality! If delivered insincerely, they may do more harm than good. Be earnest and mean what you say, or else your magical phrase may (rightly) be perceived as plain old manipulation.
- **Timing is everything**. Take a little care in how you embed these phrases into conversation. Make it natural and make it flow. Sometimes, you may need to make small adjustments to tone and phrasing to better suit your audience.

Provided you follow these few simple rules, these magical phrases are practically guaranteed to work, every time.

Validation and Warmth

The right words can instantly make people feel good.

The right words speak directly to the universal human need for warmth, safety, and calm. **Every person alive craves validation and warmth**. They want to feel like they matter, like they have value, and like their contribution belongs in the world.

You may be surprised at just how easy it is to make them feel this way. No flattery necessary!

Phrases:

1. "I hear you."
2. "That makes sense."
3. "I get where you're coming from."
4. "You're absolutely right."
5. "That's a smart way to put it."
6. "I appreciate you sharing that."
7. "I'd feel the same way."
8. "That's a fair point."

Rogers & Farson (1957) conducted pioneering studies into the art of active listening and found that any time someone is able to both **reflect** and **validate** what they hear, it increases trust, reduces defensiveness, and improves communication overall. Similarly, Reis & Shaver's *Interpersonal Process Model of Intimacy* (1988) explains how relationships tend to deepen quickly when people feel validated.

The more responsive and warm you are, the more likeable and trustworthy you will seem.

Being seen, heard, and understood is a fundamental human need. We all crave it. You can tap into this need by simply using the above phrases. The other person may not necessarily be able to say *why*, but they'll feel safer and more respected in your company.

Curiosity and Engagement

This set of phrases is about making the conversation itself feel good. Interactions can stall and stagnate if there isn't enough energy or interest to drive it along. **Conversations need to move**—there needs to be a lively back and forth.

And what makes them move? Curiosity.

To make conversations feel fun, relevant, and interesting—to make them feel worth having in the first place—you need to use language that invites disclosure, sparks interest, and demonstrate your attentive care. A well-considered question does all that.

Phrases:

1. "Tell me more."
2. "And then what happened?"
3. "What's the story behind that?"
4. "How did that feel for you?"
5. "That's fascinating—how did that come about?"

6. "What surprised you most?"
7. "What do you like best about it?"
8. "Why do you think that worked?"

You'll recall that Aron et. al.'s "36 Questions" were essentially curiosity-based questions that dramatically accelerated intimacy. We've seen that appropriate self-disclosure is a demonstration of risk-taking and vulnerability, which increases feelings of trust and liking. But any question you ask will encourage the other person to make an emotional investment of their own, and follow-up questions are especially good.

Kashdan et al. (2011) find that the presence of curiosity predicts stronger interpersonal bonds and higher relationship satisfaction. People who show genuine interest are rated as more enjoyable conversational partners and more likable. The key word there, of course, is *genuine*!

Likability Boosters

Finally, we can use a special set of phrases that actually serve a secret purpose. On the surface, they appear to be highly flattering and complimentary to the other person, but in effect, they work to make *you* seem far more likeable.

Phrases:

1. "That's a great question."
2. "I admire how you handled that."

3. "You've got good taste."
4. "I like the way you think."
5. "That's actually really inspiring."
6. "I'd trust your take on that."
7. "You always notice the details."
8. "I respect that approach."

One of the quirks of human conversation is that people tend to like those that like them. Byrne (1971) explored what is called the Similarity-Attraction Effect, which suggests that **people are more attracted to those who validate or affirm traits they identify with**.

More recently, Gonzaga and colleagues (2001) found that expressions of admiration and appreciation create positive emotions, which in turn strengthen feelings of bondedness.

Even tiny affirmations ("I love that," or "Good insight,") are **perceived as social rewards**, making people like and trust you more. In essence, you are conditioning them—training them, even, to associate interacting with you with good feelings. They're more drawn to you because interacting with you feels intrinsically *rewarding*!

Does the person you're talking to care about knowledge and learning? Compliment their taste in books. Do they clearly take a lot of pride in their high standards and hard work? Say, "Wow, you make it look so easy." Is it obvious that being a parent is a big part of their identity?

Say, "As a parent you probably already know all this, but..."

You'll make them feel good, but you'll simultaneously make *yourself* look good.

Conclusion

Struggling socially can be stressful and discouraging, but you're not alone!

Take heart that social skills are just that—skills. And skills can be acquired. With patience, practice, and a little self-compassion, we can take an honest inventory of our social strengths and weaknesses, and apply evidence-based techniques to start getting better results.

The first step is to confirm that we're not jeopardizing our conversations with eight common but deadly conversation mistakes, including "boomerasking" and failing to ask open, follow-up questions.

The underlying issue with all eight of these mistakes? Being overly focused on ourselves.

The solution is to make a deliberate shift of attention outwards again, onto other people.

No matter what you're struggling with the most right now, the way out is to reorient awareness, change perspective, and dismantle any beliefs that are limiting you.

Social skills are skills—but underneath those skills lies a particular attitude; a healthy and flexible way of looking at things. It's about:

- Less ego, more real confidence
- Less anxiety, more resilience

- Less self-absorption, more curiosity about others
- Less self-importance, more appreciation
- Less conflict, more chemistry
- Less control, more presence

We've explored many common social struggles in this book, but in every case, shifting attention outwards and tapping into this healthier mindset allows us to identify simple, practical solutions going forward.

Let's recap.

Do you freeze up in conversations? You're likely overestimating how much people are scrutinizing you.

- Remember that conversation is not a performance.
- Turn attention outwards—listen actively or pay attention to your external environment.
- Ask questions—more of them than you think!

Hate small talk? Start seeing small talk as a door and a necessary first step.

- Learn to create ladders of gently escalating self-disclosure.

Feel unlikeable? Your perception is probably distorted.

- Turn your attention away from internal flaws, and outwards, actively looking for evidence that people are engaging with you.

Feel awkward meeting strangers? It's normal! If social anxiety is getting out of hand, use CBT principles to gradually expose yourself to your social fears, without reaching for your emotional crutches.

- Remember: Avoidance reinforces anxiety. Approaching what you fear diminishes that fear.
- Excessive, inward-turning self-focus intensifies anxiety, but externalizing your attention lowers anxiety.

Don't want to "bother" people? It's another cognitive bias. People tend to appreciate our sociality more than we predict they will.

- Check in on people—more than you think you should.
- Make it an automatic habit.

Don't have opportunities to meet people? You have to deliberately engineer them for yourself.

- Joint recurrent, activity-based groups, paying special attention to weak ties.

Are new friendships not sticking? They're fragile. Consistently take the initiative and maintain a regular check-in schedule.

- Draw clear boundaries and limits for yourself when it comes to flakiness
- But don't be a flake yourself!

Do conversations feel lopsided? Imbalance can be a problem, but the solution might not be what you think.

- *Generally*, the more people speak, the more likeable they are.
- That said, it's not about how much you *talk*, it's about how much you *contribute*.

Bad at social cues? You can get better with practice.

- Start small and work your way up.
- Turn attention outwards and observe expressions of open vs. closed, tense vs. relaxed, advancing vs. retreating, etc.

Do people mistake your shyness for rudeness? You may need to actively push against this phenomenon.

- Deliberately signal warmth, interest, and liking.
- Give compliments, be grateful, offer praise, and be honest about how you feel.
- If you're a "tell it like it is" person, remember that truth matters, but how you tell the truth matters, too.
- **Before speaking, ask:**
- Is it actually true?

o   Is it useful or helpful?
o   Is it kind?
o   Does it need to be said?
o   Does it need to be said by me?
o   Does it need to be said right now?

Often forget names and details? It's an innocent mistake, but it can erode feelings of trust and connection, and make people feel unimportant.

- You may not have a memory problem, but an attention problem. Be more present, alert, and mindful.
- Use memory devices, mnemonics, imagery, and association to better encode new memories.

Hate group conversations? They require a different skill set than one-on-one conversations—for example being a little louder, bolder and more concise.

- Try activity-first groups, where it's easier to jump in and make yourself heard.
- Adjust your expectations, be graceful about interruptions, and use groups strategically to build one-on-one connections.

Don't want to network? The trick is to reframe it not as *transactional*, but *relational*.

- Find, Remind, and Bind—strategically use gratitude to locate, prompt, and reinforce reciprocal value exchanges.

- Like all relationships, networking is about gradually building rapport and trust.

Never progress beyond acquaintance level? Don't rely on chemistry, good intentions, or compatibility alone.

- Consistent and conscious effort is what progresses relationships—think cooking, not chemistry.
- Progressive self-disclosure moves the friendship to the next level, but keep disclosures small, balanced, and appropriate.

Do disagreements get out of hand? Shift attention outwards and go into active listening mode. Don't make the Shift.

- First, adopt the attitude that the other person is worthy, that you respect them, and that you are genuinely curious about their perspective.
- From there, use listening skills like reflection, paraphrasing, and follow-up questions.

Small social battery? It's OK. Each of us has our own social rhythm and preference.

- Social encounters don't have to be prolonged or intense to be effective, and there are many different ways to get our socializing fix.

Long-distance friendships fizzling out? Sadly, they can, unless there is a mutual effort at ongoing maintenance.

- Recognize that long-distance friendships need to change—successful ones are not built on chance, but by choice.
- Make an effort, adapt, and check in on a schedule.
- Recognize that not every friendship lasts a lifetime. Some are built on convenience and proximity, and when circumstances change, so do they.

Feel awkward approaching strangers? You can train yourself to be a master at engaging new people.

- Understand how rejection sensitivity works and push against it.
- Use behavioral experiments to challenge and rewrite your assumptions and expectations.
- Remember: Avoidance makes fear worse, but gradual exposure dissolves it. Build tolerance in tiny, easy-to-manage ways.

Have trouble trusting people? Controlled self-disclosure can help you build healthy trust in others.

- Trust is both a precondition and an outcome. It's built slowly, progressively, and in a balanced way.

- Remember that if connection and intimacy are a theme park, then trust and vulnerability are the entrance fee. To master the art of intimacy we need to learn to proactively regulate risk and exposure.

Can't find your people? They're out there—find them by engaging in values-based activities.

- Close friends are important. But so are casual friends, weak ties, and acquaintances. A solid friendship group has a little bit of everything in it!
- Similarity is overrated. Instead, look for shared core values, and don't underestimate the power of complementarity, proximity, and familiarity.

A healthy, well-functioning social life is a beautiful thing, but it takes time to cultivate.

Be patient with yourself and others, be practical, and don't be afraid to engage in a little trial and error! Almost everyone struggles socially at some point or other. But take just one small, conscious steps in the right direction, and you can begin to build on your strengths as you gently let go of thought patterns that are no longer working for you.

Will there be moments of awkwardness? Absolutely. But learning anything new feels clumsy at first... the trick is to keep going and give yourself the chance to find your flow.

Author and savant Daniel Tammet puts it like this: "I consider social skills a bit like learning a language. I've been practising it for so long over so many years I've almost lost my accent."